THE POWER OF LOVE

Understanding and Cultivating Love in Your Life

Dr. Maxwell Shimba

Printed by Shimba Publishing LLC
Printed in the United States of America

SHIMBA
PUBLISHING

TABLE OF CONTENTS

INTRODUCTION

The Power of Love

Love is perhaps the most profound and complex emotion known to humanity. It transcends cultural boundaries, religious doctrines, and social norms, manifesting in countless ways across the globe. From the gentle caress of a mother comforting her child to the passionate embrace of lovers reunited, love is an integral part of the human experience. Its power to heal, transform, and uplift is unparalleled, making it a central theme in literature, art, and philosophy throughout history.

The Universality of Love

One of the most remarkable aspects of love is its universality. Regardless of where we come from, our backgrounds, or our personal beliefs, love is a common thread that binds us all. It is a language that needs no translation, an experience that resonates with every heart. This universality is beautifully captured in the words of the ancient Greek philosopher Plato, who said, "At the touch of love, everyone becomes a poet." Indeed, love inspires us to express our deepest emotions, to connect with others, and to find meaning in our lives.

The Healing Power of Love

Love has an extraordinary capacity to heal. Whether it is the physical healing that comes from the care and attention of loved ones or the emotional healing that arises from feeling understood and accepted, love can mend wounds that seem otherwise insurmountable. Scientific research supports this notion, showing that individuals who feel loved and supported tend to recover more quickly from illness and experience lower levels of stress and anxiety. Love, in its many forms, acts as a balm for the soul, promoting overall well-being and resilience.

The Transformative Nature of Love

Love is also a powerful agent of transformation. It has the ability to change individuals, relationships, and even entire communities. On a personal level, love can inspire people to become the best versions of themselves, to grow, and to strive for greater heights. Romantic love, in particular, often brings out qualities such as patience, empathy, and selflessness, as individuals seek to nurture and support their partners.

In relationships, love fosters deeper connections and understanding. It encourages open communication, trust, and mutual respect, laying the foundation for lasting bonds. In a broader context, love can unite people across divides, fostering peace and harmony. Movements driven by love and compassion, such as those led by Mahatma Gandhi and Martin Luther King Jr., have brought about significant social change, demonstrating the profound impact love can have on the world.

The Uplifting Power of Love

Love has the power to uplift us, to fill our lives with joy and purpose. It brings light to our darkest moments, providing hope and inspiration. Whether it is the unconditional love of a parent, the companionship of a friend, or the deep connection of a romantic partner, love enriches our lives in immeasurable ways. It gives us a sense of belonging and reminds us that we are not alone.

Furthermore, love motivates us to act with kindness and generosity, to reach out to others, and to make a positive difference in the world. Acts of love, no matter how small, have a ripple effect, spreading joy and compassion far beyond the initial gesture. This uplifting power of love is beautifully encapsulated in the words of Mother Teresa: "Not all of us can do great things. But we can do small things with great love."

Exploring the Dimensions of Love

In this book, we will explore the various dimensions of love, from romantic love to parental love, and from self-love to spiritual love. Each type of love has its unique characteristics and challenges, but all share the common thread of connection and compassion. By understanding the nature of love and learning how to cultivate it in our lives, we can experience greater joy, fulfillment, and connection with others.

We will delve into the biological, psychological, and spiritual aspects of love, examining how it affects our minds, bodies, and souls. We will also provide practical tips and exercises for nurturing love in its many forms, helping you to build stronger, more loving relationships and to foster a greater sense of self-love and self-worth.

The Journey Ahead

As we embark on this journey together, let us remember that love is not just an emotion; it is a way of being. It is a choice we make every day to connect with others, to act with kindness and compassion, and to open our hearts to the beauty and wonder of life. By embracing the power of love, we can transform our lives and the world around us, creating a more loving, compassionate, and joyful existence.

In the chapters that follow, we will explore the depths of love, uncover its many facets, and learn how to harness its power to heal, transform, and uplift. Together, we will discover the true essence of love and the profound impact it can have on our lives.

DR. MAXWELL SHIMBA

CHAPTER 01

WHAT IS LOVE

Love is perhaps the most profound and complex emotion known to humanity. It transcends cultural boundaries, religious doctrines, and social norms, manifesting in countless ways across the globe. From the gentle caress of a mother comforting her child to the passionate embrace of lovers reunited, love is an integral part of the human experience. Its power to heal, transform, and uplift is unparalleled, making it a central theme in literature, art, and philosophy throughout history.

One of the most remarkable aspects of love is its universality. Regardless of where we come from, our backgrounds, or our personal beliefs, love is a common thread that binds us all. It is a language that needs no translation, an experience that resonates with every heart. This universality is beautifully captured in the words of the ancient Greek philosopher Plato, who said, "At the touch of love, everyone becomes a poet." Indeed, love inspires us to express our deepest emotions, to connect with others, and to find meaning in our lives.

The Healing Power of Love

Love has an extraordinary capacity to heal. Whether it is the physical healing that comes from the care and attention of loved ones or the emotional healing that arises from feeling understood and accepted, love can mend wounds that seem otherwise insurmountable. Scientific research supports this notion, showing that individuals who feel loved and supported tend to recover more quickly from illness and experience lower levels of stress and anxiety. Love, in its many forms, acts as a balm for the soul, promoting overall well-being and resilience.

The Transformative Nature of Love

Love is also a powerful agent of transformation. It has the ability to change individuals, relationships, and even entire communities. On a personal level, love can inspire people to become the best versions of themselves, to grow, and to strive for greater heights. Romantic love, in particular, often brings out qualities such as patience, empathy, and selflessness, as individuals seek to nurture and support their partners.

In relationships, love fosters deeper connections and understanding. It encourages open communication, trust, and mutual respect, laying the foundation for lasting bonds. In a broader context, love can unite people across divides, fostering peace and harmony. Movements driven by love and compassion, such as those led by Mahatma Gandhi and Martin Luther King Jr., have brought about significant social change, demonstrating the profound impact love can have on the world.

The Uplifting Power of Love

Love has the power to uplift us, to fill our lives with joy and purpose. It brings light to our darkest moments, providing hope and inspiration. Whether it is the unconditional love of a parent, the companionship of a friend, or the deep connection of a romantic partner, love enriches our lives in immeasurable ways. It gives us a sense of belonging and reminds us that we are not alone.

Furthermore, love motivates us to act with kindness and generosity, to reach out to others and to make a positive difference in the world. Acts of love, no matter how small, have a ripple effect, spreading joy and compassion far beyond the initial gesture. This uplifting power of love is beautifully encapsulated in the words of Mother Teresa: "Not all of us can do great things. But we can do small things with great love."

Exploring the Dimensions of Love

In this book, we will explore the various dimensions of love, from romantic love to parental love, and from self-love to spiritual love. Each type of love has its unique characteristics and challenges, but all share the common thread of connection and compassion. By understanding the nature of love and learning how to cultivate it in our lives, we can experience greater joy, fulfillment, and connection with others.

We will delve into the biological, psychological, and spiritual aspects of love, examining how it affects our minds, bodies, and souls. We will also provide practical tips and exercises for nurturing love in its many forms, helping you to build stronger, more loving relationships and foster a greater sense of self-love and self-worth.

The Journey Ahead

As we embark on this journey together, let us remember that love is not just an emotion; it is a way of being. It is a choice we make every day to connect with others, to act with kindness and compassion, and to open our hearts to the beauty and wonder of life. By embracing the power of love, we can transform our lives and the world around us, creating a more loving, compassionate, and joyful existence.

In the chapters that follow, we will explore the depths of love, uncover its many facets, and learn how to harness its power to heal, transform, and uplift. Together, we will discover the true essence of love and the profound impact it can have on our lives.

EXPLORING DIFFERENT TYPES OF LOVE

Love is an intricate and multifaceted emotion, one that has been the subject of countless poems, songs, and philosophical treatises throughout human history. While it can be challenging to define love in a way that captures all its nuances, it is possible to explore the different types of love that people experience. By understanding these various forms, we can appreciate the depth and breadth of this powerful emotion.

Romantic Love

Romantic love is perhaps the most celebrated and well-known form of love. It is the passionate, intimate connection that often forms between two people who are drawn to each other emotionally and physically. Romantic love involves a combination of intense attraction, deep affection, and a desire for mutual companionship and partnership.

Characteristics of Romantic Love:

1. Passion: Romantic love is often characterized by a strong physical and emotional attraction. This passion can

manifest as a desire to be close to a loved one, both physically and emotionally.

2. Intimacy: A key component of romantic love is the deep sense of intimacy that develops between partners. This intimacy involves sharing personal thoughts, feelings, and experiences, fostering a sense of closeness and understanding.

3. Commitment: Romantic love often involves a commitment to the relationship and to the partner. This commitment can take various forms, from dating exclusively to marriage and long-term partnerships.

4. Mutual Respect and Trust: A healthy romantic relationship is built on mutual respect and trust. Partners value each other's opinions, support each other's goals, and trust each other to be honest and faithful.

Familial Love

Familial love is the affection and bond that exists between family members. This type of love is often considered unconditional, as it persists regardless of circumstances or behavior. Familial love can include the love between parents and children, siblings, and extended family members.

Characteristics of Familial Love:

1. Unconditional Affection: Familial love is often unconditional, meaning that it is not contingent on specific

behaviors or achievements. Family members love each other simply because of their familial bond.

2. Support and Nurturing: Families provide support and nurturing, helping members grow and thrive. This support can be emotional, financial, or practical, and it fosters a sense of security and belonging.

3. Shared History and Traditions: Familial love is often strengthened by shared history and traditions. These shared experiences create a sense of continuity and connection across generations.

4. Sacrifice and Selflessness: Family members often make sacrifices for each other, putting the needs of the family above their own. This selflessness is a testament to the depth of familial love.

Platonic Love

Platonic love is the deep, affectionate bond that exists between friends. Unlike romantic love, platonic love does not involve physical attraction or romantic desire. Instead, it is characterized by a strong sense of camaraderie, mutual respect, and emotional support.

Characteristics of Platonic Love:

1. Companionship: Platonic love involves a deep sense of companionship and enjoyment of each other's company.

Friends share interests, hobbies, and activities, creating lasting memories together.

2. Mutual Support: Friends provide emotional support and encouragement, helping each other through life's challenges and celebrating each other's successes.

3. Trust and Honesty: Platonic relationships are built on trust and honesty. Friends feel comfortable sharing their thoughts and feelings, knowing they will be met with understanding and acceptance.

4. Boundaries and Respect: While platonic love involves a deep emotional connection, it also respects personal boundaries. Friends understand and respect each other's limits, ensuring a healthy and balanced relationship.

Agape Love

Agape love is often described as selfless, unconditional love. It is the kind of love that is given freely, without expecting anything in return. Agape love is considered the highest form of love, embodying compassion, altruism, and a deep sense of care for others.

Characteristics of Agape Love:

1. Selflessness: Agape love is characterized by selflessness and a willingness to put the needs of others above one's own. It involves acts of kindness and generosity without expecting anything in return.

2. Compassion: Agape love is deeply compassionate, showing empathy and understanding towards others. It involves a genuine concern for the well-being of others and a desire to alleviate their suffering.

3. Unconditional: Agape love is unconditional, meaning it is not dependent on the actions or behaviors of others. It is given freely and consistently, regardless of circumstances.

4. Universal: Agape love is universal, extending beyond personal relationships to encompass all of humanity. It is the kind of love that inspires acts of charity, social justice, and humanitarian efforts.

The Complexity of Love

While it is helpful to categorize love into different types, it is important to recognize that love is a complex and multifaceted emotion. These different forms of love often overlap and interact with each other. For example, romantic love can include elements of friendship and familial love, and familial love can encompass aspects of agape love.

Moreover, the experience of love can vary greatly from person to person. Cultural, social, and individual factors all play a role in shaping how love is expressed and experienced. Understanding these different dimensions of love can help us appreciate its complexity and depth.

Love, in all its forms, is a powerful force that shapes our lives and our relationships. By exploring the different types of love—romantic, familial, platonic, and agape—we can gain a deeper understanding of this profound emotion. Each type of love has its unique characteristics and challenges, but all share the common thread of connection and compassion. As we continue our journey through this book, we will delve deeper into these various forms of love, learning how to nurture and cultivate them in our own lives. Through this exploration, we can experience greater joy, fulfillment, and connection with others, ultimately leading to a more loving and compassionate world.

BIOLOGY OF LOVE: UNDERSTANDING THE CHEMICAL AND HORMONAL PROCESS WHAT IS LOVE

Love is not just a powerful emotion that poets and philosophers have tried to describe for centuries; it is also a complex biological process. When we fall in love, our brains and bodies undergo a series of chemical and hormonal changes that influence our feelings, behaviors, and perceptions. By understanding these processes, we can gain a deeper appreciation for the physiological underpinnings of love and how it affects us on a fundamental level.

The Role of Neurotransmitters in Love

Neurotransmitters are chemical messengers that play a crucial role in transmitting signals between neurons in the brain. Several neurotransmitters are particularly important in the experience of love:

1. Dopamine:

- Often referred to as the "pleasure chemical," dopamine is heavily involved in the reward system of the brain. When we experience something pleasurable, such as the presence of a loved one, dopamine levels increase, leading to feelings of euphoria and happiness.

- In the context of romantic love, dopamine is responsible for the intense pleasure and excitement that often accompany the early stages of a relationship. This surge of dopamine can create a sense of addiction to the loved one, driving us to seek out their company and attention.

2. Oxytocin:

- Known as the "love hormone" or "cuddle hormone," oxytocin plays a vital role in bonding and attachment. It is released in large quantities during physical touch, such as hugging, kissing, and sexual activity.

- Oxytocin promotes feelings of trust, security, and emotional closeness, strengthening the bond between partners. It also plays a significant role in parental love, particularly during childbirth and breastfeeding, fostering the connection between mother and child.

3. Serotonin:

- Serotonin is associated with mood regulation and overall well-being. In the context of love, serotonin levels can be affected, particularly during the early stages of romantic attraction.

- Interestingly, studies have shown that people in the early stages of romantic love often have lower levels of serotonin, similar to those observed in individuals with obsessive-compulsive disorder. This decrease in serotonin may explain why early romantic love can be all-consuming and lead to obsessive thoughts about the partner.

4. Norepinephrine:

- Norepinephrine, also known as noradrenaline, is involved in the body's "fight or flight" response and plays a role in the physiological arousal associated with love.

- Elevated levels of norepinephrine can lead to increased heart rate, sweaty palms, and feelings of excitement and nervousness, commonly experienced during the early stages of romantic attraction.

The Hormonal Influence on Love

In addition to neurotransmitters, several hormones play a significant role in the experience of love:

1. Testosterone and Estrogen:

- These sex hormones are involved in sexual attraction and desire. Testosterone, which is present in both men and women (though in higher levels in men), is linked to increased libido and sexual motivation.

- Estrogen, primarily present in women, also plays a role in sexual desire and reproductive behaviors. The interplay between these hormones can influence attraction and the formation of romantic relationships.

2. Vasopressin:

- Vasopressin is another hormone associated with social bonding and monogamous behaviors. It works alongside oxytocin to promote attachment and long-term commitment in romantic relationships.

- Studies on animals, particularly prairie voles, have shown that vasopressin is crucial for pair-bonding and monogamous behaviors, suggesting a similar role in human relationships.

The Brain's Love Circuitry

The experience of love is not confined to a single area of the brain; instead, it involves a complex network of regions working together:

1. The Ventral Tegmental Area (VTA):

- The VTA is a key part of the brain's reward system and is rich in dopamine-producing neurons. It is highly active during the early stages of romantic love, driving feelings of pleasure and motivation.

2. The Caudate Nucleus and Putamen:

- These structures are also part of the brain's reward system and are involved in goal-directed behaviors. They play a role in the intense focus and desire to pursue a romantic partner.

3. The Insula and Anterior Cingulate Cortex:

- These regions are involved in emotional processing and the experience of empathy. They help us understand and respond to the emotions of our loved ones, fostering emotional connection and bonding.

4. The Hypothalamus:

- The hypothalamus regulates the release of hormones such as oxytocin and vasopressin, playing a crucial role in the physical and emotional aspects of love.

Love and Long-Term Bonding

While the initial stages of love are characterized by intense passion and excitement, long-term relationships involve a different set of biological processes. As relationships mature, the brain shifts from the reward-focused circuitry of early love to regions associated with attachment and long-term bonding.

1. Transition from Passionate to Companionate Love:

- Over time, the intense passion of early love often evolves into companionate love, characterized by deep emotional intimacy, mutual respect, and long-term commitment.

- This transition is supported by the continued release of oxytocin and vasopressin, which promote bonding and attachment.

2. The Role of Endorphins:

- Endorphins, the body's natural painkillers, play a role in long-term relationships by promoting feelings of comfort and stability. The presence of a long-term partner can increase endorphin levels, contributing to a sense of well-being and security.

The biology of love is a fascinating interplay of neurotransmitters, hormones, and brain regions working together to create the complex emotions and behaviors associated with love. By understanding the chemical and hormonal processes that occur in the brain and body when we experience love, we can appreciate the profound impact this emotion has on our lives.

As we continue our exploration of love in this book, we will delve into the various forms of love, from romantic to familial to spiritual, and learn how to cultivate and nurture these relationships. Through this understanding, we can harness the power of love to heal, transform, and uplift ourselves and those around us.

THE PSYCHOLOGY OF LOVE: EXAMINING THE EMOTIONAL AND MENTAL ASPECTS

Love is a deeply emotional experience that encompasses a wide range of feelings and thoughts. Understanding the psychological underpinnings of love can help us navigate our relationships more effectively and foster deeper connections with others. In this chapter, we will explore the emotional and mental aspects of love, including attachment styles and love languages, to gain a better understanding of how love shapes our lives.

Attachment Styles

Attachment theory, developed by John Bowlby and later expanded by Mary Ainsworth, provides a framework for understanding how our early relationships with caregivers influence our patterns of attachment in adult relationships. According to attachment theory, there are four primary attachment styles: secure, anxious-preoccupied, dismissive-avoidant, and fearful-avoidant.

1. Secure Attachment:

- Individuals with a secure attachment style generally have a positive view of themselves and others. They feel comfortable with intimacy and independence, and they are able to form healthy, trusting relationships.

- Characteristics: Trust, open communication, emotional regulation, and a balance between closeness and independence.

- Impact on Relationships: Securely attached individuals are often able to build strong, supportive relationships characterized by mutual respect and affection.

2. Anxious-Preoccupied Attachment:

- Those with an anxious-preoccupied attachment style often seek high levels of intimacy, approval, and responsiveness from their partners. They may have a negative view of themselves and a positive view of others.

- Characteristics: High emotional reactivity, fear of abandonment, and a strong desire for closeness.

- Impact on Relationships: This attachment style can lead to dependency, jealousy, and relationship anxiety, making it challenging to maintain balanced relationships.

3. Dismissive-Avoidant Attachment:

- Individuals with a dismissive-avoidant attachment style tend to maintain emotional distance from others and may have a positive view of themselves but a negative view of others.

- Characteristics: Independence, self-reliance, and a tendency to avoid emotional closeness.

- Impact on Relationships: This attachment style can result in difficulty forming close connections, reluctance to rely on others, and a preference for solitude.

4. Fearful-Avoidant Attachment:

- Those with a fearful-avoidant attachment style often have mixed feelings about intimacy and closeness. They may desire close relationships but also fear getting hurt.

- Characteristics: Ambivalence, emotional turbulence, and a fear of rejection.

- Impact on Relationships: This attachment style can lead to unpredictable and tumultuous relationships, with individuals struggling to balance their desire for closeness with their fear of vulnerability.

Understanding your attachment style can provide valuable insights into your relationship patterns and help you work towards developing healthier, more secure connections with others.

Love Languages

The concept of love languages, introduced by Dr. Gary Chapman in his book "The Five Love Languages," offers a practical framework for understanding how people express and receive love. According to Chapman, there are five primary love languages: words of affirmation, acts of service, receiving gifts, quality time, and physical touch. Identifying your own love language and that of your partner can enhance communication and strengthen your relationship.

1. Words of Affirmation:

   - Individuals who prefer words of affirmation feel loved when they receive verbal expressions of affection, praise, and appreciation. Compliments, encouraging words, and affirming statements are particularly meaningful to them.

   - Examples: "I love you," "You look great today," and "I'm proud of you."

2. Acts of Service:

   - For those who value acts of service, actions speak louder than words. They feel loved when their partner does things to help them or make their life easier.

   - Examples: Doing household chores, running errands, and preparing meals.

3. Receiving Gifts:

- People who appreciate receiving gifts feel loved when they receive thoughtful presents. The value of the gift is not as important as the thought and effort behind it.

- Examples: Surprising your partner with their favorite snack, giving a meaningful piece of jewelry, or bringing home flowers.

4. Quality Time:

- Those who prioritize quality time feel loved when they have their partner's undivided attention. Spending time together, engaging in meaningful conversations, and sharing activities are important to them.

- Examples: Going on a walk together, having a date night, or simply sitting and talking without distractions.

5. Physical Touch:

- Individuals who prefer physical touch feel loved through physical expressions of affection. Hugs, kisses, holding hands, and other forms of physical contact are particularly meaningful to them.

- Examples: Cuddling on the couch, giving a back rub, or holding hands while walking.

Emotional and Mental Aspects of Love

In addition to attachment styles and love languages, several other psychological factors play a role in the experience of love:

1. Emotional Intimacy:

- Emotional intimacy involves sharing personal thoughts, feelings, and experiences with a partner. It requires vulnerability and trust, creating a deep sense of connection and understanding.

- Building emotional intimacy: Engage in open and honest communication, practice active listening, and express empathy and support.

2. Empathy:

- Empathy is the ability to understand and share the feelings of another person. It is a crucial component of healthy relationships, fostering emotional closeness and mutual respect.

- Cultivating empathy: Practice putting yourself in your partner's shoes, validate their emotions, and respond with compassion.

3. Conflict Resolution:

- Conflict is a natural part of any relationship, but how it is handled can significantly impact the relationship's health. Effective conflict resolution involves addressing disagreements constructively and finding mutually satisfying solutions.

- Strategies for conflict resolution: Stay calm, focus on the issue at hand, communicate openly, and seek compromise.

4. Emotional Regulation:

- Emotional regulation is the ability to manage and respond to one's emotions in a healthy way. It is essential for maintaining stability and harmony in relationships.

- Enhancing emotional regulation: Practice mindfulness, develop healthy coping mechanisms, and seek professional help if needed.

The psychology of love encompasses a wide range of emotional and mental aspects that influence how we experience and express love. By understanding attachment styles, love languages, and other psychological factors, we can gain valuable insights into our relationship patterns and work towards building healthier, more fulfilling connections with others.

As we continue our exploration of love in this book, we will delve into the various forms of love, including romantic, familial, and spiritual love. Through this journey, we can learn how to harness the power of love to heal, transform, and uplift ourselves and those around us, ultimately leading to a more loving and compassionate world.

THEOLOGY OF LOVE: A CHRISTIAN PERSPECTIVE

Love is central to the Christian faith. It is the essence of God's character and the foundation of His relationship with humanity. In this chapter, we will explore the theology of love from a Christian perspective, drawing on biblical texts and expository studies to understand how love is portrayed in the Bible and how it shapes the lives of believers.

The Nature of God's Love

The Bible describes God as the very embodiment of love. This is profoundly stated in 1 John 4:8: "Whoever does not love does not know God, because God is love." This verse encapsulates the essence of God's character—love is not merely an attribute of God; it is His very nature.

1. Unconditional Love (Agape):

 - Agape love is the highest form of love, characterized by selflessness, sacrificial giving, and unconditional commitment. God's love for humanity is the ultimate example of agape love.

 - Romans 5:8: "But God demonstrates his own love for us in this: While we were still sinners, Christ died for us."

This verse highlights the sacrificial nature of God's love, demonstrating that His love is given freely, without condition.

2. Everlasting Love:

- God's love is eternal and unchanging. It is not based on our actions or worthiness but on His character and promises.

- Jeremiah 31:3: "The Lord appeared to us in the past, saying: 'I have loved you with an everlasting love; I have drawn you with unfailing kindness.'" This verse reassures believers of the permanence and steadfastness of God's love.

3. Personal and Intimate Love:

- God's love is personal and intimate, reaching out to each individual with care and compassion.

- Psalm 139:1-3: "You have searched me, Lord, and you know me. You know when I sit and when I rise; you perceive my thoughts from afar. You discern my going out and my lying down; you are familiar with all my ways." This passage reflects the depth of God's personal knowledge and love for each person.

The Command to Love

The Bible not only reveals God's love for us but also commands us to love others. This commandment is central to Christian ethics and is seen as a reflection of God's love in our lives.

1. The Greatest Commandment:

- Jesus emphasized the importance of love in the greatest commandment, which encapsulates the essence of all the Law and the Prophets.

- Matthew 22:37-40: "Jesus replied: 'Love the Lord your God with all your heart and with all your soul and with all your mind.' This is the first and greatest commandment. And the second is like it: 'Love your neighbor as yourself.' All the Law and the Prophets hang on these two commandments." This passage underscores the comprehensive nature of love, encompassing our relationship with God and with others.

2. Love One Another:

- Jesus' new commandment calls believers to love one another as He has loved us.

- John 13:34-35: "A new command I give you: Love one another. As I have loved you, so you must love one another. By this everyone will know that you are my disciples, if you love one another." This commandment highlights the transformative power of love in the Christian community and its role in witnessing to the world.

The Expression of Love in the Christian Life

Love is not merely a feeling but is expressed through actions and attitudes. The Bible provides numerous examples and exhortations on how to live out love in practical ways.

1. Self-Sacrificial Love:

- Following the example of Christ, believers are called to live lives of self-sacrificial love.

- John 15:13: "Greater love has no one than this: to lay down one's life for one's friends." This verse challenges believers to demonstrate love through selfless actions and willingness to sacrifice for others.

2. Love in Action:

- Love is demonstrated through tangible actions that meet the needs of others.

- 1 John 3:18: "Dear children, let us not love with words or speech but with actions and in truth." This verse emphasizes that genuine love is active and practical, going beyond mere words.

3. Patient and Kind Love:

- The famous "love chapter" in 1 Corinthians 13 provides a comprehensive description of what love looks like in action.

- 1 Corinthians 13:4-7: "Love is patient, love is kind. It does not envy, it does not boast, it is not proud. It does not dishonor others, it is not self seeking, it is not easily angered, it keeps no record of wrongs. Love does not delight in evil but rejoices with the truth. It always protects, always trusts, always hopes, always perseveres." This passage outlines the attributes of love and serves as a guide for believers in their relationships.

Love as the Fulfillment of the Law

The New Testament teaches that love is the fulfillment of the law. All commandments are summed up in the command to love.

1. Love and the Law:

- Romans 13:8-10: "Let no debt remain outstanding, except the continuing debt to love one another, for whoever loves others has fulfilled the law. The commandments, 'You shall not commit adultery,' 'You shall not murder,' 'You shall not steal,' 'You shall not covet,' and whatever other command there may be, are summed up in this one command: 'Love your neighbor as yourself.' Love does no harm to a neighbor. Therefore love is the fulfillment of the law." This passage explains that love is the guiding principle that fulfills all moral and ethical requirements.

The Transformative Power of Love

Love has the power to transform individuals and communities. Through love, believers can reflect the character of God and bring about positive change in the world.

1. Transforming Relationships:

- Colossians 3:12-14: "Therefore, as God's chosen people, holy and dearly loved, clothe yourselves with compassion, kindness, humility, gentleness and patience. Bear with each other and forgive one another if any of you has a grievance against someone. Forgive as the Lord forgave you. And over all these virtues put on love, which binds them all together in perfect unity." This passage illustrates how love can transform relationships by fostering virtues that promote unity and harmony.

2. Impacting the World:

- 1 John 4:11-12: "Dear friends, since God so loved us, we also ought to love one another. No one has ever seen God; but if we love one another, God lives in us and his love is made complete in us." This verse emphasizes the role of love in making God's presence known in the world through the lives of believers.

The theology of love in the Christian faith is rich and multifaceted. It encompasses the nature of God's love, the command to love others, and the practical expression of love in the lives of believers. By understanding and embracing this theology, Christians can experience the transformative power of love and reflect God's character in their relationships and communities.

As we continue our exploration of love in this book, we will delve into the various forms of love, including romantic, familial, and spiritual love. Through this journey, we can learn how to harness the power of love to heal, transform, and uplift ourselves and those around us, ultimately leading to a more loving and compassionate world.

CHAPTER 02

THE IMPORTANCE OF LOVE

Love and Health: Exploring the Impact of Love on Our Physical and Mental Well-Being

Love is often celebrated for its emotional and spiritual significance, but its impact extends far beyond feelings and relationships. Scientific research has increasingly shown that love plays a crucial role in our physical and mental health. In this chapter, we will explore how love influences our well-being, examining both the physiological and psychological benefits of being loved and loving others.

The Physical Benefits of Love

1. Cardiovascular Health:

- Love and affection have been linked to better heart health. Engaging in loving relationships can lower blood pressure, reduce stress, and decrease the risk of cardiovascular diseases.

- Studies have shown that people in supportive, loving relationships have lower levels of stress hormones such as cortisol, which can lead to a healthier heart. A study published in the American Journal of Cardiology found that married individuals or those in stable, loving relationships had a lower risk of heart disease compared to their single counterparts.

2. Boosted Immune System:

- Love and social connections can strengthen the immune system, making the body more resilient against illnesses. Positive social interactions and emotional bonds can lead to the release of beneficial hormones that boost immunity.

- A study from Carnegie Mellon University found that people with strong social ties and supportive relationships were less likely to catch colds and had a more robust immune response to infections.

3. Pain Management:

- Love and affection can also play a role in pain management. Physical touch, such as hugging, holding hands, or cuddling, can trigger the release of oxytocin, often referred to as the "love hormone."

- Oxytocin has been shown to reduce pain perception and increase pain tolerance. In a study published in the journal Pain, participants who held their partner's hand reported feeling less pain than those who did not.

4. Longevity:

- Engaging in loving relationships can contribute to a longer life. Studies have shown that individuals who are married or have strong social connections tend to live longer than those who are isolated or lonely.

- Research from Brigham Young University found that social relationships can improve survival rates by 50%, highlighting the significant impact of love and connection on longevity.

The Mental Health Benefits of Love

1. Reduced Stress and Anxiety:

- Love and affectionate relationships can significantly reduce stress and anxiety levels. Being in a supportive relationship provides a sense of security and belonging, which can help mitigate the effects of stress.

- A study published in the journal Psychosomatic Medicine found that individuals in happy, loving relationships had lower levels of cortisol, the stress hormone, compared to those in less supportive relationships.

2. Improved Mood and Happiness:

- Love has a profound impact on mood and overall happiness. Positive social interactions and emotional bonds can increase the production of neurotransmitters such as dopamine and serotonin, which are associated with feelings of happiness and well-being.

- A study in the Journal of Social and Personal Relationships found that people in loving relationships reported higher levels of life satisfaction and happiness compared to those who were single or in unhappy relationships.

3. Enhanced Emotional Resilience:

- Love and social support can enhance emotional resilience, helping individuals cope better with life's challenges and setbacks. Knowing that there are people who care for and support us provides a buffer against the negative effects of stress and adversity.

- Research published in the Journal of Personality and Social Psychology found that people with strong social support networks were more resilient and better able to cope with major life stressors.

4. Reduced Risk of Mental Health Disorders:

- Engaging in loving relationships can reduce the risk of mental health disorders such as depression and anxiety. The sense of connection and support provided by loving relationships can act as a protective factor against these conditions.

- A meta-analysis published in the journal PLOS Medicine found that individuals with strong social relationships had a 50% increased likelihood of survival and a lower risk of mental health disorders compared to those with weaker social ties.

The Impact of Different Types of Love

1. Romantic Love:

- Romantic love, characterized by passion, intimacy, and commitment, can have profound effects on both physical and mental health. The initial stages of romantic love can lead to increased energy, improved mood, and a sense of euphoria.

- However, the benefits of romantic love extend beyond the initial "honeymoon phase." Long-term, committed relationships provide emotional stability, security, and companionship, all of which contribute to overall well-being.

2. Familial Love:

- Familial love, encompassing the bonds between parents, children, and siblings, plays a critical role in emotional development and mental health. The unconditional support and care provided by family members can foster a sense of belonging and self-worth.

- Research has shown that strong family bonds are associated with lower levels of depression and anxiety, as well as better overall mental health.

3. Platonic Love:

- Platonic love, or the affection between friends, is equally important for mental and physical health. Friendships provide companionship, support, and a sense of belonging, all of which contribute to well-being.

- A study published in the journal Personal Relationships found that close friendships were associated with increased happiness and life satisfaction, as well as lower levels of stress and anxiety.

4. Self-Love:

- Self-love, or the practice of self-compassion and self-care, is essential for overall well-being. Cultivating a positive self-image and treating oneself with kindness and respect can improve mental health and resilience.

- Research published in the journal Clinical Psychology Review found that self-compassion was associated with lower levels of anxiety and depression, as well as greater life satisfaction and emotional resilience.

Practical Tips for Cultivating Love and Enhancing Well-Being

1. Nurture Relationships:

- Invest time and effort in building and maintaining strong, loving relationships. Prioritize quality time with loved ones, communicate openly and honestly, and show appreciation and affection regularly.

2. Practice Self-Love:

- Cultivate self-love by engaging in self-care activities, setting healthy boundaries, and practicing self-compassion. Treat yourself with the same kindness and understanding that you would offer to a close friend.

3. Express Gratitude:

- Regularly express gratitude for the people in your life and the love you receive. Practicing gratitude can enhance positive emotions and strengthen relationships.

4. Engage in Physical Touch:

- Physical touch, such as hugging, holding hands, or cuddling, can boost oxytocin levels and promote feelings of connection and well-being. Don't underestimate the power of a warm embrace.

5. Foster Emotional Intimacy:

- Build emotional intimacy by sharing your thoughts, feelings, and experiences with loved ones. Practice active listening and empathy to deepen your connections.

Love is a powerful force that significantly impacts our physical and mental well-being. From reducing stress and anxiety to boosting immune function and promoting longevity, the benefits of love are far-reaching and profound. By understanding the importance of love and actively cultivating it in our lives, we can enhance our health, happiness, and overall quality of life.

As we continue our exploration of love in this book, we will delve into the various forms of love, including romantic, familial, and spiritual love. Through this journey, we can learn how to harness the power of love to heal, transform, and uplift ourselves and those around us, ultimately leading to a more loving and compassionate world.

LOVE AND RELATIONSHIP

How Love Contributes to Healthy, Fulfilling Relationships

Love is the cornerstone of all meaningful relationships. Whether it's the bond between family members, the intimacy shared between romantic partners, or the connection between friends, love plays a pivotal role in creating and sustaining healthy, fulfilling relationships. In this chapter, we will explore the various ways love contributes to relationship health and fulfillment, examining key elements such as communication, trust, respect, and emotional support.

The Foundation of Love in Relationships

1. Mutual Respect:

- Respect is fundamental to any healthy relationship. It involves recognizing and valuing each other's individuality, opinions, and boundaries.

- When love is present, respect naturally follows. Partners who love each other will honor each other's feelings and viewpoints, fostering an environment where both parties feel valued and understood.

2. Trust:

- Trust is the bedrock of all strong relationships. It allows individuals to feel safe and secure, knowing that their partner is reliable and has their best interests at heart.

- Love nurtures trust by promoting honesty, transparency, and fidelity. When partners trust each other, they are more likely to share their vulnerabilities and work through challenges together.

3. Communication:

- Effective communication is crucial for maintaining a healthy relationship. It involves not only expressing one's thoughts and feelings but also actively listening to and understanding the partner's perspective.

- Love enhances communication by encouraging openness and empathy. Loving partners are more inclined to engage in constructive dialogue, resolve conflicts amicably, and support each other's emotional needs.

4. Emotional Support:

- Emotional support is a key aspect of a fulfilling relationship. It involves being there for each other during times of joy and sorrow, offering comfort, encouragement, and understanding.

- Love provides the foundation for emotional support, fostering a sense of connection and empathy that allows partners to navigate life's ups and downs together.

Love in Romantic Relationships

1. Intimacy and Connection:

- Intimacy is a hallmark of romantic relationships, encompassing both physical closeness and emotional bonding. It involves sharing one's innermost thoughts, feelings, and experiences with a partner.

- Love fuels intimacy by creating a safe space where partners can be vulnerable and authentic. This deep connection strengthens the bond between partners and enhances relationship satisfaction.

2. Passion and Desire:

- Passion is a key component of romantic love, characterized by physical attraction and a desire for closeness. It adds excitement and energy to the relationship.

- Love sustains passion by fostering a strong emotional connection and mutual admiration. Partners who love each other are more likely to maintain a vibrant and satisfying physical relationship.

3. Commitment and Loyalty:

- Commitment is the decision to remain dedicated to the relationship and to work through challenges together. It involves loyalty, perseverance, and a long-term perspective.

- Love underpins commitment by creating a strong emotional bond that motivates partners to invest in the relationship and overcome obstacles.

Love in Familial Relationships

1. Unconditional Support:

- Familial love is often unconditional, providing a stable source of support and security. Family members are there for each other through thick and thin, offering a reliable foundation of care and affection.

- This unconditional support is rooted in love, which fosters a sense of belonging and safety within the family unit.

2. Nurturing and Guidance:

- Love plays a crucial role in nurturing and guiding family members, especially children. It involves providing care, protection, and encouragement to help individuals grow and thrive.

- Parents who love their children create an environment that promotes healthy development, self-esteem, and resilience.

3. Conflict Resolution:

- Conflict is a natural part of any family dynamic, but love helps to navigate and resolve disagreements constructively. Loving family members are more likely to approach conflicts with empathy and a desire for reconciliation.

- This commitment to resolving conflicts peacefully strengthens family bonds and fosters a harmonious home environment.

Love in Friendships

1. Companionship and Joy:

- Friendships are enriched by love, which brings joy, companionship, and shared experiences. Friends who love each other enjoy spending time together and create lasting memories.

- This companionship and joy are integral to maintaining a fulfilling and supportive friendship.

2. Loyalty and Trustworthiness:

- Love in friendships is characterized by loyalty and trustworthiness. Friends who love each other stand by one another, offering support and solidarity in times of need.

- This loyalty creates a strong and dependable bond that withstands the test of time.

3. Mutual Growth and Encouragement:

- Loving friends encourage each other's personal growth and development. They celebrate each other's successes, offer constructive feedback, and motivate each other to pursue their goals.

- This mutual growth and encouragement are essential for a fulfilling and enriching friendship.

Practical Tips for Cultivating Love in Relationships

1. Prioritize Quality Time:

- Invest time and effort in nurturing your relationships. Spend quality time with loved ones, engage in meaningful conversations, and participate in activities that strengthen your bond.

2. Practice Active Listening:

- Show genuine interest in your partner's thoughts and feelings. Practice active listening by giving your full attention, asking open-ended questions, and responding with empathy.

3. Express Appreciation and Gratitude:

- Regularly express appreciation and gratitude for your loved ones. Acknowledge their positive qualities and the things they do for you, and let them know how much they mean to you.

4. Show Affection:

- Demonstrate your love through physical affection, kind words, and thoughtful gestures. Small acts of love and kindness can have a significant impact on your relationship.

5. Communicate Openly and Honestly:

- Maintain open and honest communication with your loved ones. Share your thoughts and feelings openly, and encourage your partner to do the same.

6. Resolve Conflicts Constructively:

- Approach conflicts with a willingness to understand and find common ground. Focus on the issue at hand, avoid blame, and work together to find a solution.

Love is the foundation of healthy, fulfilling relationships. It fosters mutual respect, trust, effective communication, and emotional support, all of which are essential for building and maintaining strong connections with others. By understanding the role of love in relationships and actively cultivating it, we can create more meaningful and enriching bonds with our partners, family members, and friends.

As we continue our exploration of love in this book, we will delve into the various forms of love, including self-love and spiritual love. Through this journey, we can learn how to harness the power of love to heal, transform, and uplift ourselves and those around us, ultimately leading to a more loving and compassionate world.

LOVE AND SOCIETY

Examining the Role of Love in Building Strong, Compassionate Communities

Love extends beyond personal relationships and plays a vital role in shaping the fabric of society. It is the driving force behind compassion, empathy, and cooperation, essential qualities for creating strong and compassionate communities. In this chapter, we will explore how love influences societal structures and interactions, promoting unity, social justice, and collective well-being.

The Foundation of Love in Society

1. Compassion and Empathy:

   - Compassion and empathy are fundamental components of love that enable individuals to understand and share the feelings of others. These qualities foster a sense of connectedness and solidarity within a community.

- Compassionate communities are more likely to support their members in times of need, creating a network of care and assistance that strengthens social bonds.

2. Social Cohesion:

- Love promotes social cohesion by encouraging individuals to work together for the common good. It fosters a sense of belonging and mutual responsibility, which are essential for maintaining harmony and cooperation within a community.

- When love guides social interactions, communities are more likely to develop inclusive and supportive environments where everyone feels valued and respected.

3. Altruism and Volunteerism:

- Altruism, or selfless concern for the well-being of others, is a manifestation of love that drives people to engage in acts of kindness and generosity. Volunteerism is a practical expression of altruism, where individuals contribute their time and resources to help others.

- Communities with a strong culture of volunteerism are more resilient and better equipped to address social challenges, as members actively participate in creating positive change.

Love and Social Justice

1. Advocacy and Activism:

- Love is a powerful motivator for social justice advocacy and activism. It inspires individuals to fight against inequality, discrimination, and injustice, striving to create a fairer and more equitable society.

- Historical movements for civil rights, gender equality, and LGBTQ+ rights have been driven by love and compassion for marginalized and oppressed groups, highlighting the transformative power of love in achieving social justice.

2. Building Inclusive Communities:

- Love encourages the creation of inclusive communities where diversity is celebrated, and everyone has equal opportunities to thrive. It challenges prejudices and promotes acceptance, understanding, and respect for differences.

- Inclusive communities are more cohesive and harmonious, as they recognize and value the unique contributions of all their members, fostering a sense of unity and shared purpose.

3. Support for Vulnerable Populations:

- Love drives individuals and organizations to support vulnerable populations, such as the homeless, refugees, and those living in poverty. Compassionate actions, such as providing shelter, food, and healthcare, are essential for addressing the needs of these groups.

- By prioritizing the well-being of the most vulnerable, communities can create a more just and equitable society where everyone has the opportunity to lead a dignified life.

Love in Civic Engagement

1. Fostering Civic Responsibility:

- Love for one's community and fellow citizens fosters a sense of civic responsibility. Individuals who care deeply about their community are more likely to engage in civic activities, such as voting, participating in local government, and supporting community initiatives.

- Civic engagement strengthens democratic processes and ensures that the voices of all community members are heard and considered in decision-making.

2. Promoting Cooperative Efforts:

- Love promotes cooperation and collaboration among community members. When people work together towards common goals, they can achieve greater outcomes and address complex social issues more effectively.

- Cooperative efforts, such as community clean-up projects, neighborhood watch programs, and local fundraising events, exemplify how love can unite people to create positive change.

3. Encouraging Social Connectedness:

- Social connectedness is crucial for mental and emotional well-being. Love fosters strong social networks, providing individuals with a sense of belonging and support.

- Communities that prioritize social connectedness are more resilient and better equipped to face challenges, as members can rely on each other for assistance and encouragement.

Love and Global Citizenship

1. Promoting Global Awareness:

- Love extends beyond local communities to encompass global citizenship. It encourages individuals to care about global issues, such as climate change, human rights, and international development.

- By fostering a sense of global awareness and responsibility, love motivates people to take actions that contribute to the well-being of the global community.

2. Encouraging Cultural Exchange:

- Love promotes cultural exchange and understanding, helping to bridge gaps between different cultures and societies. It encourages individuals to appreciate and learn from diverse perspectives, fostering mutual respect and cooperation.

- Cultural exchange initiatives, such as student exchange programs, international collaborations, and cultural festivals, highlight the role of love in creating a more interconnected and harmonious world.

3. Supporting Humanitarian Efforts:

- Humanitarian efforts, driven by love and compassion, address global challenges such as poverty, natural disasters, and conflict. These efforts provide essential aid and support to those in need, demonstrating the power of love to transcend borders and make a difference.

- Organizations such as the Red Cross, Doctors Without Borders, and UNICEF exemplify how love can mobilize resources and expertise to address global crises and promote human welfare.

Practical Tips for Fostering Love in Society

1. Promote Kindness and Generosity:

- Encourage acts of kindness and generosity within your community. Small gestures, such as helping a neighbor, volunteering, or donating to a local charity, can have a significant impact on creating a culture of love and compassion.

2. Support Inclusive Policies:

- Advocate for inclusive policies and practices that promote equality and social justice. Support initiatives that address the needs of marginalized groups and work towards creating a more equitable society.

3. Engage in Community Building:

- Participate in community-building activities, such as neighborhood events, local projects, and civic organizations. Building strong social networks and fostering a sense of community can enhance social cohesion and collective well-being.

4. Educate and Raise Awareness:

- Raise awareness about important social issues and educate others about the importance of love and compassion in creating positive change. Use your platform to advocate for social justice and promote a culture of empathy and understanding.

5. Practice Active Listening and Empathy:

- Engage in active listening and empathetic communication with others. Understanding different perspectives and experiences can foster deeper connections and promote a more compassionate society.

Love is a powerful force that shapes the fabric of society. It promotes compassion, empathy, and cooperation, essential qualities for building strong, inclusive, and compassionate communities. By understanding the role of love in society and actively cultivating it, we can create a more just and equitable world where everyone has the opportunity to thrive.

As we continue our exploration of love in this book, we will delve into the various forms of love, including romantic, familial, and spiritual love. Through this journey, we can learn how to harness the power of love to heal, transform, and uplift ourselves and those around us, ultimately leading to a more loving and compassionate world.

CHAPTER 03

CULTIVATING SELF-LOVE

Understanding Self-Love: Exploring the Importance of Self-Compassion and Self-Acceptance

Self-love is a foundational element of overall well-being and healthy relationships. It involves recognizing and embracing your intrinsic worth, showing compassion towards yourself, and accepting yourself as you are. Cultivating self-love is essential for leading a fulfilling and balanced life. In this chapter, we will explore the importance of self-compassion and self-acceptance, and provide practical steps to develop and nurture self-love.

The Concept of Self-Love

Self-love is not about narcissism or self-absorption; rather, it is about treating yourself with the same kindness, respect, and care that you would offer to a loved one. It means acknowledging your strengths and weaknesses, celebrating your achievements, and forgiving yourself for mistakes.

1. Self-Compassion:

- Self-compassion involves being kind and understanding towards yourself, especially during times of difficulty or failure. It means recognizing that suffering, failure, and imperfection are part of the human experience and responding with care and empathy.

- According to Dr. Kristin Neff, a leading researcher on self-compassion, this concept encompasses three main components: self-kindness, common humanity, and mindfulness.

2. Self-Acceptance:

- Self-acceptance is about embracing all aspects of yourself, including your flaws and imperfections. It involves recognizing your intrinsic worth and valuing yourself regardless of external achievements or validation.

- Self-acceptance is crucial for building self-esteem and resilience, as it provides a stable foundation of self-worth that is not dependent on external circumstances.

The Importance of Self-Compassion

1. Emotional Resilience:

- Self-compassion enhances emotional resilience by providing a source of inner strength and support. When you are kind to yourself, you are better equipped to cope with challenges and setbacks.

   - Research has shown that self-compassion is associated with lower levels of anxiety, depression, and stress, and higher levels of emotional well-being and life satisfaction.

2. Improved Mental Health:

   - Self-compassion is linked to better mental health outcomes. By treating yourself with kindness and understanding, you can reduce negative self-talk and self-criticism, which are major contributors to mental health issues.

   - Studies have found that self-compassion can reduce symptoms of depression, anxiety, and PTSD, and promote overall psychological well-being.

3. Healthy Relationships:

   - Self-compassion fosters healthy relationships by promoting a positive self-image and reducing dependency on external validation. When you are compassionate towards yourself, you are less likely to seek approval from others and more likely to form balanced and fulfilling relationships.

   - Being kind to yourself also allows you to extend compassion and empathy to others, creating a more loving and supportive social environment.

The Importance of Self-Acceptance

1. Authentic Self-Expression:

   - Self-acceptance allows you to express yourself authentically without fear of judgment or rejection. When you accept yourself as you are, you can pursue your passions, goals, and values with confidence and integrity.

   - Authentic self-expression leads to greater fulfillment and a deeper sense of purpose in life.

2. Increased Self-Esteem:

   - Self-acceptance is the foundation of healthy self-esteem. When you value and accept yourself, you build a stable sense of self-worth that is not dependent on external achievements or validation.

   - High self-esteem is associated with greater confidence, resilience, and overall well-being.

3. Reduced Self-Judgment:

   - Self-acceptance reduces self-judgment and the constant need to compare yourself to others. By embracing your unique qualities and imperfections, you can let go of unrealistic standards and expectations.

   - This leads to greater peace of mind and a more positive self-image.

Practical Steps to Cultivate Self-Love

1. Practice Self-Compassion:

- Treat yourself with kindness and understanding, especially during times of difficulty. Speak to yourself in a gentle and supportive manner, just as you would to a friend.

- Use self-compassionate phrases such as "It's okay to feel this way," "I'm doing my best," and "I deserve care and kindness."

2. Engage in Self-Care:

- Prioritize self-care activities that nourish your body, mind, and spirit. This can include exercise, healthy eating, sufficient rest, hobbies, and relaxation techniques.

- Make time for activities that bring you joy and fulfillment, and set boundaries to protect your well-being.

3. Challenge Negative Self-Talk:

- Become aware of negative self-talk and challenge these thoughts with positive affirmations and self-compassionate statements.

- Replace self-criticism with constructive and supportive inner dialogue. For example, instead of saying, "I'm such a failure," say, "I made a mistake, but I can learn from it and improve."

4. Practice Mindfulness:

- Mindfulness involves being present in the moment and observing your thoughts and feelings without judgment.

Practicing mindfulness can help you develop a more compassionate and accepting attitude towards yourself.

- Engage in mindfulness practices such as meditation, deep breathing, and mindful observation of your surroundings.

5. Celebrate Your Achievements:

- Acknowledge and celebrate your achievements, no matter how small. Take time to reflect on your accomplishments and give yourself credit for your efforts and successes.

- Create a gratitude journal where you write down things you are proud of and grateful for in your life.

6. Surround Yourself with Positive Influences:

- Surround yourself with people who support and uplift you. Build a social network of individuals who encourage your growth and well-being.

- Limit exposure to negative influences and environments that undermine your self-worth and self-acceptance.

7. Seek Professional Support:

- If you struggle with self-compassion and self-acceptance, consider seeking support from a therapist or counselor. Professional guidance can help you develop healthier thought patterns and self-care practices.

- Therapy can provide a safe space to explore and address underlying issues that may be affecting your self-love.

Cultivating self-love is essential for leading a fulfilling and balanced life. By practicing self-compassion and self-acceptance, you can build a strong foundation of self-worth, resilience, and well-being. Understanding and embracing your intrinsic value allows you to navigate life's challenges with greater confidence and authenticity, ultimately leading to healthier relationships and a more compassionate outlook on life.

As we continue our exploration of love in this book, we will delve into the various forms of love, including romantic, familial, and spiritual love. Through this journey, we can learn how to harness the power of love to heal, transform, and uplift ourselves and those around us, ultimately leading to a more loving and compassionate world.

OVERCOMING BARRIERS TO SELF-LOVE

Overcoming Barriers to Self-Love: Addressing Common Obstacles Such as Self-Criticism and Perfectionism

Self-love is a crucial component of well-being and healthy relationships, but it is often obstructed by internal and external barriers. Self-criticism and perfectionism are two of the most common obstacles that can hinder our ability to love and accept ourselves. In this chapter, we will explore these barriers in depth and provide practical strategies for overcoming them, enabling you to cultivate a more compassionate and loving relationship with yourself.

Understanding Self-Criticism

Self-criticism involves harshly judging and condemning oneself for perceived flaws, mistakes, or shortcomings. It is a destructive inner dialogue that undermines self-esteem and fosters feelings of inadequacy and unworthiness.

1. Origins of Self-Criticism:

- Self-criticism often stems from early life experiences, such as critical parenting, societal pressures, and negative feedback from peers. These experiences can shape our self-perception and create a habit of internalized criticism.

- Perfectionism, societal expectations, and comparison with others can exacerbate self-critical tendencies.

2. Impact of Self-Criticism:

- Self-criticism can lead to mental health issues such as depression, anxiety, and low self-esteem. It can also hinder personal growth and prevent us from pursuing our goals and dreams.

- Negative self-talk erodes self-worth and creates a cycle of shame and self-doubt, making it difficult to practice self-love.

Overcoming Self-Criticism

1. Develop Self-Awareness:

- The first step in overcoming self-criticism is to develop self-awareness. Pay attention to your inner dialogue and identify self-critical thoughts.

- Exercise: Keep a journal to track instances of self-criticism. Note the triggers, the content of the thoughts, and the emotions they evoke.

2. Challenge Negative Thoughts:

- Challenge self-critical thoughts by examining their validity and replacing them with more balanced and compassionate perspectives.

- Exercise: When you notice a self-critical thought, ask yourself, "Is this thought true?" "Is there evidence to support this thought?" and "What would I say to a friend in a similar situation?"

3. Practice Self-Compassion:

- Treat yourself with the same kindness and understanding that you would offer to a loved one. Respond to self-critical thoughts with self-compassionate statements.

- Exercise: When you catch yourself being self-critical, pause and say, "I am doing my best," "It's okay to make mistakes," or "I deserve kindness and compassion."

4. Reframe Mistakes as Learning Opportunities:

- Instead of viewing mistakes as failures, reframe them as opportunities for growth and learning. Embrace a growth mindset that values progress over perfection.

- Exercise: Reflect on a recent mistake and write down what you learned from the experience and how it can help you grow.

Understanding Perfectionism

Perfectionism is the relentless pursuit of flawlessness and the belief that anything less than perfect is unacceptable. It is often driven by fear of failure, fear of judgment, and a desire for external validation.

1. Origins of Perfectionism:

- Perfectionism can arise from early life experiences, such as high parental expectations, societal pressures, and a culture that values achievement and success.

- It is often reinforced by societal messages that equate self-worth with accomplishments and external validation.

2. Impact of Perfectionism:

- Perfectionism can lead to chronic stress, anxiety, and burnout. It creates unrealistic standards that are impossible to meet, resulting in constant feelings of inadequacy and failure.

- Perfectionism can also hinder creativity, spontaneity, and personal fulfillment, as it focuses on outcomes rather than the joy of the process.

Overcoming Perfectionism

1. Set Realistic Goals:

- Set realistic and achievable goals that are based on your values and capabilities. Avoid setting overly high standards that set you up for failure.

- Exercise: Break down larger goals into smaller, manageable steps. Celebrate your progress and acknowledge your achievements along the way.

2. Embrace Imperfection:

- Embrace the idea that imperfection is a natural and inherent part of being human. Recognize that mistakes and flaws do not diminish your worth.

- Exercise: Identify an area of your life where you feel the pressure to be perfect. Allow yourself to make mistakes and be imperfect in that area, and observe how it feels.

3. Focus on the Process:

- Shift your focus from the outcome to the process. Find joy and fulfillment in the journey rather than fixating on the end result.

- Exercise: Engage in a creative activity without the goal of perfection. Allow yourself to experiment, make mistakes, and enjoy the process.

4. Practice Self-Compassion:

- Cultivate self-compassion by treating yourself with kindness and understanding when you fall short of your expectations. Recognize that everyone experiences setbacks and failures.

- Exercise: When you feel the urge to be perfect, pause and say, "I am enough just as I am," "I am worthy of love and acceptance," or "It is okay to be imperfect."

Additional Strategies for Overcoming Barriers to Self-Love

1. Surround Yourself with Supportive People:

- Surround yourself with people who uplift and support you. Seek out relationships that encourage self-love and self-acceptance.

- Exercise: Identify supportive friends and family members who reinforce positive self-talk and self-compassion. Spend more time with these individuals and limit exposure to those who perpetuate self-criticism and perfectionism.

2. Limit Comparisons:

- Avoid comparing yourself to others, as comparisons often fuel self-criticism and perfectionism. Focus on your own unique journey and progress.

- Exercise: When you catch yourself comparing, remind yourself that everyone has their own path and timeline. Celebrate your individuality and accomplishments.

3. Seek Professional Support:

- If self-criticism and perfectionism are deeply ingrained and challenging to overcome, consider seeking support from a therapist or counselor. Professional guidance can help you develop healthier thought patterns and coping strategies.

- Exercise: Find a therapist who specializes in self-esteem, self-compassion, or cognitive-behavioral therapy (CBT) to address these issues.

4. Engage in Mindfulness Practices:

- Mindfulness practices, such as meditation and deep breathing, can help you become more aware of your thoughts and emotions and develop a more compassionate attitude towards yourself.

- Exercise: Practice mindfulness meditation for a few minutes each day. Focus on your breath and observe your thoughts without judgment.

Overcoming barriers to self-love, such as self-criticism and perfectionism, is essential for developing a healthy and compassionate relationship with yourself. By cultivating self-awareness, challenging negative thoughts, practicing self-compassion, and embracing imperfection, you can break free from these obstacles and nurture a greater sense of self-love and self-worth.

As we continue our exploration of love in this book, we will delve into the various forms of love, including romantic, familial, and spiritual love. Through this journey, we can learn how to harness the power of love to heal, transform, and uplift ourselves and those around us, ultimately leading to a more loving and compassionate world.

CHAPTER 04

NATURING ROMANTIC LOVE

Building a Strong Foundation: The Importance of Communication, Trust, and Mutual Respect in Romantic Relationships

Romantic love is a profound and enriching experience that can bring immense joy and fulfillment. However, nurturing a healthy and lasting romantic relationship requires effort and commitment. Building a strong foundation is essential for sustaining love over time. In this chapter, we will explore the key elements of a solid foundation in romantic relationships: communication, trust, and mutual respect. By understanding and prioritizing these components, couples can create a loving and supportive partnership that endures.

The Role of Communication in Romantic Relationships

1. Open and Honest Communication:

- Open and honest communication is the cornerstone of a healthy romantic relationship. It involves expressing thoughts, feelings and needs clearly and authentically.

- When partners communicate openly, they create an environment of transparency and trust, where both individuals feel heard and understood.

2. Active Listening:

- Active listening is a critical aspect of effective communication. It involves fully focusing on the speaker, understanding their message, and responding thoughtfully.

- By practicing active listening, partners demonstrate empathy and validation, which strengthens their emotional connection.

3. Nonverbal Communication:

- Nonverbal communication, such as body language, facial expressions, and tone of voice, plays a significant role in conveying emotions and intentions.

- Being mindful of nonverbal cues helps partners interpret each other's feelings accurately and respond with sensitivity.

4. Conflict Resolution:

- Conflicts are inevitable in any relationship, but how they are handled can make a significant difference.

Effective communication during conflicts involves staying calm, avoiding blame, and focusing on finding solutions.

- Exercise: Practice "I" statements during disagreements (e.g., "I feel hurt when...") to express feelings without assigning blame, and work together to find mutually agreeable resolutions.

Building Trust in Romantic Relationships

1. Reliability and Consistency:

- Trust is built on reliability and consistency. Partners need to demonstrate dependability through their actions, showing that they can be counted on to keep promises and commitments.

- Exercise: Follow through on commitments, be punctual, and show up for your partner in meaningful ways to build trust over time.

2. Transparency and Honesty:

- Honesty and transparency are crucial for fostering trust. Being open about thoughts, feelings, and experiences helps partners understand each other better and builds a foundation of trust.

- Exercise: Share your daily experiences, dreams, and concerns with your partner, and encourage them to do the same. Create a safe space for open and honest conversations.

3. Trustworthiness:

- Trustworthiness involves being truthful and maintaining integrity. Trust is damaged when partners are deceitful or betray each other's confidence.

- Exercise: Practice honesty in all interactions, and avoid behaviors that could erode trust, such as lying or withholding important information.

4. Forgiveness and Rebuilding Trust:

- Trust can be broken, but it can also be rebuilt through forgiveness and consistent efforts to regain trust. Forgiveness involves letting go of past grievances and working towards healing.

- Exercise: If trust has been broken, engage in open dialogue about the issue, express genuine remorse, and commit to actions that rebuild trust over time.

The Importance of Mutual Respect in Romantic Relationships

1. Valuing Each Other's Individuality:

- Mutual respect involves valuing each other's individuality and differences. Recognize and appreciate your partner's unique qualities, perspectives, and contributions to the relationship.

- Exercise: Celebrate your partner's achievements and strengths, and encourage their personal growth and interests.

2. Equality and Fairness:

- Respect in a relationship means treating each other as equals and ensuring fairness in decision-making and responsibilities. Avoid power imbalances and work towards a balanced partnership.

- Exercise: Share responsibilities equitably, make joint decisions and ensure that both partners have an equal say in matters that affect the relationship.

3. Boundaries and Personal Space:

- Respecting each other's boundaries and personal space is essential for maintaining a healthy relationship. Recognize and honor your partner's need for independence and privacy.

- Exercise: Communicate your boundaries clearly and listen to your partner's boundaries. Respect each other's need for alone time and personal pursuits.

4. Appreciation and Gratitude:

- Expressing appreciation and gratitude reinforces mutual respect and strengthens the emotional bond. Regularly acknowledge and thank your partner for their efforts and contributions.

- Exercise: Make a habit of expressing gratitude daily. Write down or verbally share three things you appreciate about your partner each day.

Practical Tips for Nurturing Romantic Love

1. Quality Time Together:

- Prioritize quality time together to nurture your relationship. Engage in activities that you both enjoy and create meaningful experiences.

- Exercise: Schedule regular date nights, weekend getaways, or simply spend time together without distractions to strengthen your bond.

2. Affection and Intimacy:

- Physical affection and emotional intimacy are vital for maintaining a strong romantic connection. Show affection through hugs, kisses, and other forms of physical touch, and nurture emotional closeness through deep conversations and shared experiences.

- Exercise: Set aside time for physical affection and intimate conversations. Make an effort to connect on both physical and emotional levels regularly.

3. Support and Encouragement:

- Be a source of support and encouragement for your partner. Celebrate their successes, provide comfort during challenges, and show that you are there for them unconditionally.

- Exercise: Offer words of encouragement and acts of support. Be present during important moments and show empathy and understanding.

4. Shared Goals and Values:

- Aligning on shared goals and values strengthens the partnership and creates a sense of unity. Discuss your aspirations, dreams, and values, and work together towards common objectives.

- Exercise: Have regular discussions about your long-term goals and values. Create a vision board together or set mutual goals to work towards as a couple.

Nurturing romantic love requires building a strong foundation based on communication, trust, and mutual respect. By prioritizing open and honest communication, cultivating trust through reliability and transparency, and showing mutual respect by valuing each other's individuality and boundaries, couples can create a loving and supportive partnership that endures.

As we continue our exploration of love in this book, we will delve into the various forms of love, including familial and spiritual love. Through this journey, we can learn how to harness the power of love to heal, transform, and uplift ourselves and those around us, ultimately leading to a more loving and compassionate world.

KEEPING THE SPARK ALIVE

Tips for Maintaining Passion and Intimacy in Long-Term Relationships

Long-term relationships bring a sense of stability, deep connection, and mutual understanding. However, maintaining the passion and intimacy that characterize the early stages of a relationship can be challenging as time goes on. It is essential to continually nurture and invest in your relationship to keep the spark alive. In this chapter, we will explore practical tips and strategies for maintaining passion and intimacy in long-term relationships.

Understanding the Nature of Passion and Intimacy

1. The Evolution of Love:

- Romantic relationships often begin with intense passion and excitement. This initial phase, sometimes referred to as the "honeymoon phase," is characterized by heightened emotions, physical attraction, and novelty.

- As relationships mature, the intensity of these initial feelings may diminish, but this does not mean that passion and intimacy cannot be sustained. Instead, love evolves into a deeper, more stable connection that requires ongoing effort to maintain.

2. The Importance of Intimacy:

- Intimacy in a relationship goes beyond physical closeness; it encompasses emotional, intellectual, and experiential connection. It involves sharing your innermost thoughts, feelings, and experiences with your partner.

- Maintaining intimacy is crucial for a fulfilling relationship, as it fosters trust, empathy, and a sense of security.

Tips for Maintaining Passion and Intimacy

1. Prioritize Quality Time Together:

- Spending quality time together is essential for keeping the spark alive. Make an effort to engage in activities that you both enjoy and that allow you to connect on a deeper level.

- Exercise: Schedule regular date nights, weekend getaways, or simply spend uninterrupted time together at home. The key is to create opportunities for meaningful connections.

2. Keep the Romance Alive:

- Small romantic gestures can have a significant impact on maintaining passion in a relationship. Thoughtful actions, surprises, and expressions of love can reignite the romance.

- Exercise: Surprise your partner with a love note, plan a special dinner, or give them a thoughtful gift. Regularly express your love and appreciation in creative ways.

3. Communicate Openly and Honestly:

- Open and honest communication is vital for maintaining intimacy. Share your thoughts, feelings, and desires with your partner, and encourage them to do the same.

- Exercise: Set aside time for regular check-ins where you can discuss your relationship, express your needs, and address any concerns. Practice active listening and empathy during these conversations.

4. Explore New Experiences Together:

- Engaging in new and exciting activities together can help reignite passion and create shared memories. Novel experiences stimulate the brain and can enhance the bond between partners.

- Exercise: Try new hobbies, travel to new places, or take on new challenges together. The goal is to break the routine and introduce fresh excitement into your relationship.

5. Maintain Physical Affection:

- Physical affection is a crucial component of intimacy and helps reinforce the emotional connection between partners. Regular touch, hugs, kisses, and cuddling can strengthen your bond.

- Exercise: Make physical affection a daily habit. Whether it's holding hands, giving a massage, or simply cuddling on the couch, these small acts of touch can keep the connection strong.

6. Cultivate Emotional Intimacy:

- Emotional intimacy involves sharing your inner world with your partner and being receptive to theirs. This deepens your understanding and strengthens your emotional bond.

- Exercise: Engage in deep conversations where you share your dreams, fears, and aspirations. Be vulnerable and open, and create a safe space for your partner to do the same.

7. Keep the Sexual Connection Alive:

- A healthy sexual relationship is an important aspect of maintaining passion and intimacy. Prioritize physical intimacy and make an effort to keep the sexual connection vibrant.

- Exercise: Communicate openly about your sexual needs and desires. Experiment with new ways to enhance your sexual intimacy, such as trying new activities or exploring fantasies together.

8. Show Appreciation and Gratitude:

- Regularly expressing appreciation and gratitude can reinforce positive feelings and strengthen your relationship. Acknowledge the efforts and qualities of your partner that you value.

- Exercise: Make a habit of expressing gratitude daily. Tell your partner what you appreciate about them and how much they mean to you.

9. Practice Forgiveness and Let Go of Grudges:

- Holding onto past grievances can create distance and resentment in a relationship. Practice forgiveness and work towards resolving conflicts constructively.

- Exercise: When conflicts arise, address them calmly and seek resolution. Let go of grudges and focus on moving forward together with a positive mindset.

10. Invest in Personal Growth:

- Personal growth and self-improvement can positively impact your relationship. When both partners are committed to their own growth, it enhances the overall dynamic of the relationship.

- Exercise: Pursue your interests, set personal goals, and support each other in your individual journeys. Celebrate each other's achievements and growth.

Overcoming Challenges in Maintaining Passion and Intimacy

1. Addressing Routine and Boredom:

- Routine and predictability can sometimes lead to boredom in a relationship. To counteract this, actively seek out new and stimulating activities that bring excitement and novelty.

- Exercise: Plan spontaneous dates or surprise outings. Introduce new experiences that break the monotony and create fresh excitement.

2. Dealing with Stress and External Pressures:

- External stressors, such as work, family responsibilities, or financial pressures, can impact your relationship. It's important to support each other and find ways to manage stress together.

- Exercise: Practice stress-relief techniques such as meditation, exercise, or hobbies that you both enjoy. Communicate openly about the stressors you're facing and work together to find solutions.

3. Reconnecting After Drift:

- It's natural for couples to experience periods of emotional drift. Recognize when this happens and take proactive steps to reconnect and rebuild intimacy.

- Exercise: Plan a dedicated time to reconnect, such as a weekend retreat or a special date night. Engage in activities that promote closeness and re-establish emotional connection.

4. Navigating Differences:

- Differences in interests, personalities, or life goals can create challenges. Embrace these differences as opportunities for growth and understanding.

- Exercise: Engage in open and respectful discussions about your differences. Find common ground and work together to navigate any conflicts that arise.

Keeping the spark alive in a long-term relationship requires ongoing effort, intentionality, and a commitment to nurturing the connection between partners. By prioritizing quality time, maintaining open communication, exploring new experiences, and showing appreciation, couples can sustain passion and intimacy over the long term.

As we continue our exploration of love in this book, we will delve into the various forms of love, including familial and spiritual love. Through this journey, we can learn how to harness the power of love to heal, transform, and uplift ourselves and those around us, ultimately leading to a more loving and compassionate world.

OVERCOMING CHALLENGES

Navigating Common Issues Such as Conflict, Jealousy, and Infidelity

Every relationship encounters challenges, and how couples navigate these issues can significantly impact the health and longevity of their partnership. Conflict, jealousy, and infidelity are among the most common and potentially destructive challenges. In this chapter, we will explore strategies for addressing and overcoming these issues, helping couples to strengthen their bond and maintain a healthy, fulfilling relationship.

Navigating Conflict

Conflict is a natural part of any relationship. Differences in opinions, values, and preferences can lead to disagreements. However, conflicts do not have to be detrimental. When handled constructively, they can strengthen the relationship.

1. Understanding Conflict:

   - Conflict arises from differences in needs, desires, and perspectives. It is important to recognize that conflict is not inherently negative; it is an opportunity for growth and understanding.

2. Effective Communication:

- Open and respectful communication is key to resolving conflicts. Use "I" statements to express your feelings and needs without blaming your partner.

- Exercise: Practice active listening during conflicts. Allow your partner to speak without interruption, and then reflect back on what you heard to ensure understanding.

3. Staying Calm:

- Emotions can run high during conflicts, making it difficult to think clearly. Take a moment to calm down before addressing the issue.

- Exercise: Practice deep breathing or take a short break to cool off if you feel overwhelmed during a disagreement.

4. Finding Common Ground:

- Focus on finding a solution that satisfies both partners' needs. Compromise and collaboration are essential for resolving conflicts.

- Exercise: Make a list of potential solutions together and discuss the pros and cons of each. Choose a solution that works for both of you.

5. Avoiding Personal Attacks:

- Personal attacks and name-calling can escalate conflicts and cause lasting harm. Focus on the issue at hand rather than attacking your partner's character.

- Exercise: Set ground rules for fair fighting, such as no yelling, name-calling, or bringing up past grievances.

Dealing with Jealousy

Jealousy can stem from insecurity, fear of loss, or perceived threats to the relationship. While a certain amount of jealousy is natural, excessive jealousy can erode trust and create tension.

1. Understanding Jealousy:

- Recognize the underlying causes of jealousy. It often reflects deeper insecurities or fears rather than actual threats to the relationship.

2. Open Communication:

- Discuss your feelings of jealousy openly and honestly with your partner. Avoid accusatory language and focus on expressing your own emotions and concerns.

- Exercise: Use statements like, "I feel jealous when..." to start the conversation and explain your feelings without blaming your partner.

3. Building Trust:

- Strengthen trust in your relationship by being reliable, honest, and transparent. Trust is built over time through consistent and trustworthy behavior.

- Exercise: Share your daily activities with your partner and be open about your interactions with others to foster transparency.

4. Addressing Insecurities:

- Work on building your self-esteem and addressing personal insecurities. Feeling confident and secure in yourself can reduce feelings of jealousy.

- Exercise: Engage in activities that boost your self-confidence and self-worth. Seek support from a therapist if needed.

5. Setting Boundaries:

- Establish clear boundaries in your relationship to prevent situations that may trigger jealousy. Mutual respect for these boundaries is crucial.

- Exercise: Have a discussion about what behaviors and interactions are comfortable for both of you and agree on boundaries that protect your relationship.

Overcoming Infidelity

Infidelity is one of the most challenging issues a relationship can face. It involves a breach of trust that can cause deep emotional pain. However, with commitment and effort, couples can work through infidelity and rebuild their relationship.

1. Understanding the Impact:

\- Infidelity has a profound impact on both partners and the relationship. It is important to acknowledge the pain and betrayal felt by the injured partner.

2. Open Communication:

\- Honest and open communication is essential for healing after infidelity. The unfaithful partner must be willing to answer questions and provide transparency.

\- Exercise: Schedule regular check-ins to discuss feelings, progress, and any lingering concerns. Create a safe space for honest conversations.

3. Seeking Professional Help:

\- Couples therapy can provide a supportive environment to work through the complex emotions and issues related to infidelity. A therapist can help guide the healing process.

\- Exercise: Commit to attending therapy sessions together and actively participate in the process.

4. Rebuilding Trust:

\- Rebuilding trust takes time and consistent effort. The unfaithful partner must demonstrate accountability, honesty, and a commitment to change.

- Exercise: Create a plan for rebuilding trust, including specific actions and behaviors that show commitment and transparency.

5. Forgiveness and Moving Forward:

- Forgiveness is a crucial step in healing, but it is a process that takes time. Both partners must be willing to let go of the past and work towards a new beginning.

- Exercise: Practice forgiveness exercises, such as writing letters of forgiveness or participating in guided forgiveness meditations.

Additional Strategies for Overcoming Relationship Challenges

1. Regular Relationship Check-Ins:

- Schedule regular check-ins to discuss the state of your relationship, address any concerns, and celebrate successes.

- Exercise: Set aside time each month for a relationship check-in. Use this time to discuss what is working well and what areas need attention.

2. Prioritize Self-Care:

- Taking care of your own mental and emotional well-being is essential for a healthy relationship. Prioritize self-care activities that help you stay balanced and resilient.

- Exercise: Engage in regular self-care practices, such as exercise, meditation, hobbies, or spending time with friends and family.

3. Strengthen Emotional Connection:

- Deepen your emotional connection by sharing your inner thoughts, dreams, and fears. Vulnerability fosters intimacy and strengthens the bond between partners.

- Exercise: Set aside time for deep conversations and emotional sharing. Use prompts like, "What is something you have always wanted to share with me?" to start meaningful dialogues.

4. Celebrate Milestones and Achievements:

- Celebrate your relationship milestones and achievements. Acknowledging your journey together reinforces your commitment and appreciation for each other.

- Exercise: Plan special celebrations for anniversaries, birthdays, and other significant events. Reflect on your shared experiences and express gratitude for your partnership.

Overcoming challenges such as conflict, jealousy, and infidelity requires effort, commitment, and a willingness to grow together. By practicing effective communication, building trust, and showing mutual respect, couples can navigate these issues and strengthen their relationship.

Remember that seeking professional help and prioritizing self-care are also important steps in maintaining a healthy and fulfilling partnership.

As we continue our exploration of love in this book, we will delve into the various forms of love, including familial and spiritual love. Through this journey, we can learn how to harness the power of love to heal, transform, and uplift ourselves and those around us, ultimately leading to a more loving and compassionate world.

CHAPTER 05

EMBRACING FAMILIA LOVE

The Unique Bond of Family: Exploring the Dynamics of Parent-Child Relationships, Sibling Relationships, and Extended Family Connections

Familial love is a powerful and unique bond that shapes our identity, values, and experiences. It is within the family unit that we first learn about love, trust, and connection. The dynamics of familial relationships are complex and multifaceted, encompassing parent-child relationships, sibling relationships, and extended family connections. In this chapter, we will explore these different aspects of familial love, highlighting their significance and providing insights into nurturing and strengthening these bonds.

The Parent-Child Relationship

1. Unconditional Love and Support:

- The parent-child relationship is often characterized by unconditional love and support. Parents provide a foundation of care and security that is essential for a child's development.

- This unconditional love fosters a sense of belonging and self-worth, helping children grow into confident and compassionate individuals.

2. Nurturing and Guidance:

- Parents play a crucial role in nurturing and guiding their children. This includes providing physical care, emotional support, and moral guidance.

- Effective parenting involves balancing discipline with affection, setting boundaries while encouraging independence, and being a positive role model.

3. Open Communication:

- Open and honest communication is vital for a healthy parent-child relationship. It fosters trust, understanding, and emotional connection.

- Exercise: Create regular opportunities for open dialogue with your child. Encourage them to express their thoughts and feelings, and listen actively without judgment.

4. Quality Time and Shared Activities:

- Spending quality time together strengthens the parent-child bond. Shared activities create lasting memories and provide opportunities for connection and learning.

- Exercise: Plan regular family activities such as game nights, outdoor adventures, or cooking together. These moments of shared joy and connection are invaluable.

5. Encouragement and Affirmation:

- Positive reinforcement and affirmation are essential for building a child's self-esteem and confidence. Celebrate their achievements, big and small, and offer words of encouragement.

- Exercise: Make a habit of acknowledging your child's efforts and accomplishments. Use phrases like, "I'm proud of you," and "You did a great job."

The Sibling Relationship

1. Companionship and Friendship:

- Siblings often provide companionship and friendship throughout life. This bond can be a source of support, fun, and shared experiences.

- Encourage positive interactions and cooperation between siblings to foster a strong and lasting relationship.

2. Navigating Sibling Rivalry:

- Sibling rivalry is common and can arise from competition for attention, resources, or approval. It is important to address and manage these conflicts constructively.

- Exercise: Teach conflict resolution skills and encourage open communication. Promote fairness and avoid favoritism to minimize rivalry.

3. Shared Memories and Traditions:

- Shared memories and family traditions strengthen sibling bonds. These experiences create a sense of continuity and connection.

- Exercise: Create and uphold family traditions, such as holiday celebrations, family vacations, or special rituals. These traditions become cherished memories that siblings carry into adulthood.

4. Supporting Each Other:

- Siblings can be a source of emotional and practical support. Encourage siblings to look out for each other, offer help when needed, and celebrate each other's successes.

- Exercise: Foster a culture of support and encouragement within the family. Teach siblings to express appreciation and gratitude for each other.

The Extended Family Connection

1. Intergenerational Relationships:

- Extended family relationships, such as those with grandparents, aunts, uncles, and cousins, enrich the family dynamic. These intergenerational connections provide additional sources of love, wisdom, and support.

- Encourage regular interactions and involvement with extended family members to strengthen these bonds.

2. Family Gatherings and Reunions:

- Family gatherings and reunions are opportunities to reinforce extended family connections. These events celebrate the shared history and heritage of the family.

- Exercise: Organize regular family gatherings, such as holiday celebrations, reunions, or milestone events. These occasions create lasting bonds and cherished memories.

3. Cultural and Family Heritage:

- Extended family members often play a key role in preserving and passing down cultural and family heritage. This includes traditions, stories, and values that define the family's identity.

- Exercise: Engage in conversations about family history and traditions. Encourage extended family members to share stories and cultural practices with younger generations.

4. Providing Support and Stability:

- Extended family can provide additional support and stability during times of need. This includes offering emotional, financial, or practical assistance.

- Exercise: Cultivate a network of support within the extended family. Encourage family members to reach out and help each other during challenging times.

Strengthening Familial Love

1. Practice Forgiveness:

- Forgiveness is essential for maintaining healthy family relationships. Holding onto grudges or past grievances can create tension and distance.

- Exercise: Practice forgiveness by letting go of past hurts and focusing on healing and reconciliation. Engage in open and honest conversations to address and resolve conflicts.

2. Show Appreciation and Gratitude:

- Regularly expressing appreciation and gratitude reinforces positive feelings and strengthens familial bonds. Acknowledge the contributions and efforts of family members.

- Exercise: Make a habit of expressing gratitude daily. Share specific examples of how family members have made a positive impact on your life.

3. Create a Supportive Environment:

- A supportive family environment fosters love, trust, and emotional security. Encourage open communication, active listening, and mutual respect.

- Exercise: Establish family rules and values that promote a positive and supportive atmosphere. Encourage family members to express their thoughts and feelings openly.

4. Invest in Relationship Building:

- Building and maintaining strong family relationships requires time and effort. Invest in activities and practices that nurture these connections.

- Exercise: Plan regular family bonding activities, such as game nights, movie nights, or outdoor adventures. Prioritize spending quality time together.

Familial love is a unique and powerful bond that shapes our lives in profound ways. By understanding and nurturing the dynamics of parent-child relationships, sibling relationships, and extended family connections, we can create a supportive and loving family environment. Embracing familial love involves practicing forgiveness, showing appreciation, creating a supportive environment, and investing in relationship building. These efforts strengthen the bonds that unite us and create a foundation of love and support that lasts a lifetime.

As we continue our exploration of love in this book, we will delve into the various forms of love, including romantic, self-love, and spiritual love. Through this journey, we can learn how to harness the power of love to heal, transform, and uplift ourselves and those around us, ultimately leading to a more loving and compassionate world.

HEALING WOUNDS

Healing Family Wounds: Strategies for Resolving Conflicts and Building Stronger, More Loving Family Relationships

Family relationships are often the most influential connections in our lives, shaping our identity, values, and sense of belonging. However, these relationships can also be sources of deep conflict and emotional pain. Healing family wounds and resolving conflicts is essential for building stronger, more loving family relationships. In this chapter, we will explore strategies for addressing and resolving family conflicts, fostering forgiveness, and creating a foundation of love and understanding.

Understanding Family Wounds

1. Sources of Family Conflicts:

- Family conflicts can arise from various sources, including differences in values and beliefs, misunderstandings, unmet expectations, and past grievances.

- These conflicts can lead to feelings of hurt, resentment, and alienation, impacting the overall health of family relationships.

2. The Impact of Unresolved Conflicts:

- Unresolved conflicts can create ongoing tension and emotional distance within the family. They can also contribute to mental health issues such as anxiety, depression, and stress.

- Healing family wounds involves addressing these conflicts and working towards resolution and reconciliation.

Strategies for Resolving Family Conflicts

1. Open and Honest Communication:

- Effective communication is crucial for resolving conflicts and healing family wounds. This involves expressing thoughts and feelings openly and honestly, without blame or judgment.

- Exercise: Practice active listening during conversations. Allow family members to share their perspectives and validate their feelings, even if you disagree.

2. Empathy and Understanding:

- Empathy involves putting yourself in the other person's shoes and understanding their emotions and experiences.

This fosters compassion and helps bridge gaps in understanding.

- Exercise: During conflicts, take a moment to consider the other person's perspective. Ask yourself, "How might they be feeling?" and "What experiences might have led to their viewpoint?"

3. Establishing Boundaries:

- Setting healthy boundaries is essential for maintaining respect and preventing further conflict. Boundaries help define acceptable behaviors and protect emotional well-being.

- Exercise: Communicate your boundaries clearly and assertively. Encourage family members to do the same, and respect each other's boundaries.

4. Seeking Common Ground:

- Finding common ground and shared goals can help de-escalate conflicts and promote collaboration. Focus on areas of agreement and work towards mutually beneficial solutions.

- Exercise: Identify shared values and goals within the family. Use these commonalities as a foundation for resolving conflicts and building stronger relationships.

5. Conflict Resolution Techniques:

- Various conflict resolution techniques can be effective in addressing family disputes. These include mediation, negotiation, and collaborative problem-solving.

- Exercise: Engage in a structured conflict resolution process. This might involve a neutral mediator, setting ground rules for discussions, and brainstorming solutions together.

Fostering Forgiveness and Letting Go

1. The Power of Forgiveness:

- Forgiveness is a crucial step in healing family wounds. It involves letting go of anger and resentment and moving towards emotional freedom and peace.

- Exercise: Reflect on the benefits of forgiveness for your own well-being. Consider how holding onto grudges impacts your emotional health and relationships.

2. The Process of Forgiveness:

- Forgiveness is a process that takes time and effort. It involves acknowledging the hurt, understanding the reasons behind the actions, and choosing to let go of negative emotions.

- Exercise: Write a letter of forgiveness to a family member who has hurt you. You may choose to share it with them or keep it for yourself as a symbolic act of letting go.

3. Practicing Self-Forgiveness:

- Self-forgiveness is equally important in the healing process. It involves acknowledging your own mistakes, learning from them, and treating yourself with compassion.

- Exercise: Reflect on any guilt or self-blame you may be carrying. Write down positive affirmations and remind yourself that everyone makes mistakes and deserves forgiveness.

Building Stronger Family Relationships

1. Strengthening Emotional Bonds:

- Strengthening emotional bonds within the family involves creating opportunities for connection, understanding, and shared experiences.

- Exercise: Plan regular family activities that promote bonding and positive interactions. These can include family dinners, game nights, or outdoor adventures.

2. Creating a Supportive Environment:

- A supportive family environment fosters trust, respect, and emotional security. Encourage open communication, active listening, and mutual support.

- Exercise: Establish family rituals and traditions that promote a sense of unity and belonging. Encourage family members to express their thoughts and feelings openly.

3. Encouraging Positive Interactions:

- Positive interactions and expressions of love and appreciation reinforce healthy family dynamics. Make an effort to acknowledge and celebrate each other's strengths and contributions.

- Exercise: Create a "gratitude jar" where family members can write down and share things they appreciate about each other. Read the notes together regularly to reinforce positive feelings.

4. Seeking Professional Help:

- In some cases, professional help may be necessary to address deep-seated conflicts and emotional wounds. Family therapy can provide a safe space for healing and reconciliation.

- Exercise: Consider seeking the support of a licensed family therapist. Engage in therapy sessions together to work through unresolved issues and build healthier relationships.

Healing family wounds and resolving conflicts is essential for building stronger, more loving family relationships. By practicing open communication, empathy, and understanding, setting healthy boundaries, and fostering forgiveness, families can navigate conflicts and create a foundation of love and trust. Strengthening emotional bonds and creating a supportive environment further enhances the health and resilience of family relationships.

As we continue our exploration of love in this book, we will delve into the various forms of love, including romantic, self-love, and spiritual love. Through this journey, we can learn how to harness the power of love to heal, transform, and uplift ourselves and those around us, ultimately leading to a more loving and compassionate world.

HONORING OUR ANCESTORS

The Importance of Acknowledging and Honoring Our Familial Heritage

Acknowledging and honoring our ancestors is an essential aspect of understanding our identity, heritage, and place in the world. Our ancestors' lives, struggles, and achievements have shaped who we are today, and by honoring them, we connect with our roots and gain a deeper appreciation for our family history. In this chapter, we will explore the significance of honoring our ancestors and provide practical ways to acknowledge and celebrate our familial heritage.

The Significance of Honoring Our Ancestors

1. Connecting with Our Roots:

- Honoring our ancestors helps us connect with our roots, providing a sense of belonging and continuity. It allows us to understand where we come from and how our family's history has shaped our identity.

- Knowing our family history can instill a sense of pride and appreciation for the resilience, values, and traditions passed down through generations.

2. Preserving Cultural Heritage:

- Our ancestors' cultural practices, traditions, and beliefs are integral to our heritage. By honoring them, we preserve and pass on these cultural elements to future generations.

- Celebrating our cultural heritage helps maintain a rich and diverse tapestry of human experience, fostering a sense of unity and understanding among different communities.

3. Learning from the Past:

- Our ancestors' experiences, both triumphs and struggles, offer valuable lessons. Reflecting on their lives can provide insights into overcoming challenges, making informed decisions, and appreciating the sacrifices made for our benefit.

- Understanding our family's history helps us avoid repeating past mistakes and inspires us to build on the foundation laid by previous generations.

4. Fostering Family Bonds:

- Honoring our ancestors strengthens family bonds by creating a shared sense of history and identity. It encourages family members to come together, share stories, and celebrate their common heritage.

- This shared connection fosters a sense of unity, continuity, and mutual respect within the family.

Ways to Honor Our Ancestors

1. Researching Family History:

- Delving into family history through genealogical research helps uncover stories, traditions, and connections that may have been forgotten. This research can involve exploring historical records, family documents, and oral histories.

- Exercise: Create a family tree, documenting as much information as possible about your ancestors. Interview older family members to gather stories and memories that enrich your understanding of your heritage.

2. Creating a Family Archive:

- Establishing a family archive preserves important documents, photographs, and artifacts for future generations. This archive can serve as a tangible connection to your ancestors and a resource for ongoing exploration.

- Exercise: Collect and organize family documents, photographs, and heirlooms. Create digital copies to ensure preservation and share them with family members.

3. Celebrating Cultural Traditions:

- Participating in cultural traditions and rituals honors your ancestors' heritage and keeps these practices alive. This can include celebrating holidays, preparing traditional foods, and participating in cultural events.

- Exercise: Learn about and incorporate cultural traditions into your family celebrations. Teach younger generations the significance and practices of these traditions.

4. Visiting Ancestral Sites:

- Visiting places significant to your family's history, such as ancestral homes, gravesites, or regions where your ancestors lived, provides a deeper connection to your heritage.

- Exercise: Plan a family trip to visit ancestral sites. Reflect on the history and significance of these places and share the experience with your family.

5. Creating a Memorial or Tribute:

- Establishing a memorial or tribute to honor your ancestors can be a meaningful way to celebrate their lives and contributions. This could be a physical monument, a dedicated space in your home, or a virtual tribute.

- Exercise: Create a memorial or tribute for your ancestors. This could be a photo album, a dedicated shelf with family heirlooms, or an online family history blog.

6. Sharing Family Stories:

- Sharing family stories orally or through written records keeps the memory of your ancestors alive. These stories provide context, lessons, and a sense of continuity for future generations.

- Exercise: Host family gatherings where members share stories about their ancestors. Record these stories to create a family history book or digital archive.

Incorporating Ancestral Wisdom into Daily Life

1. Living Your Ancestors' Values:

- Reflecting on the values and principles upheld by your ancestors can guide your actions and decisions. Embracing these values honors their legacy and reinforces the cultural and moral foundation they provided.

- Exercise: Identify core values or principles that were important to your ancestors. Write them down and consider how you can incorporate them into your daily life.

2. Practicing Gratitude:

- Regularly expressing gratitude for the sacrifices and contributions of your ancestors fosters a sense of appreciation and connection. This practice can be a reminder of the resilience and strength that runs through your family line.

- Exercise: Include gratitude for your ancestors in your daily reflections or prayers. Acknowledge their impact on your life and express thanks for the heritage they passed down.

3. Continuing Family Traditions:

- Maintaining and adapting family traditions for contemporary life ensures that your heritage remains a living part of your family's experience. These traditions can be simple, such as family recipes, or more elaborate cultural practices.

- Exercise: Identify family traditions that are meaningful to you. Make a conscious effort to continue and adapt these traditions, involving younger generations in the process.

The Role of Ancestors in Shaping Identity

1. Building a Sense of Belonging:

- Understanding and honoring your ancestors helps build a strong sense of belonging. It connects you to a lineage and provides a sense of identity that transcends individual experiences.

- Exercise: Reflect on how your family history has shaped your identity. Write down aspects of your personality, values, or beliefs that are influenced by your heritage.

2. Navigating Life's Challenges:

- Drawing on the wisdom and experiences of your ancestors can provide guidance and strength during challenging times. Their resilience and achievements serve as inspiration and a reminder of your inner strength.

- Exercise: When facing difficulties, consider how your ancestors might have dealt with similar challenges. Draw strength from their experiences and use their stories as motivation to persevere.

3. Celebrating Diversity and Inclusivity:

- Honoring your ancestors encourages an appreciation of the diverse cultural and historical influences that shape your identity. This celebration of diversity fosters inclusivity and respect for different backgrounds and experiences.

- Exercise: Explore the diverse cultural influences in your family history. Learn about and celebrate the different traditions, languages, and customs that contribute to your heritage.

Honoring our ancestors is a profound way to connect with our roots, preserve our cultural heritage, and strengthen family bonds. By acknowledging the lives and contributions of those who came before us, we gain a deeper appreciation for our identity and place in the world. Practical steps such as researching family history, celebrating cultural traditions, and sharing family stories help keep the memory of our ancestors alive and ensure that their legacy continues to inspire and guide us.

As we continue our exploration of love in this book, we will delve into the various forms of love, including romantic, self-love, and spiritual love. Through this journey, we can learn how to harness the power of love to heal, transform, and uplift ourselves and those around us, ultimately leading to a more loving and compassionate world.

CHAPTER 06

EXPERIRNCING SPIRITUAL LOVE

Experiencing Spiritual Love: Connecting with a Higher Power

Spiritual love transcends the material world and connects us with a higher power or divine presence. It is a profound and transformative experience that can provide meaning, purpose, and inner peace. Spiritual love is expressed in various ways across different spiritual traditions, each offering unique perspectives on connecting with the divine and experiencing the boundless love of a higher power. In this chapter, we will explore how love is expressed in various spiritual traditions and how these practices can enrich our lives.

The Nature of Spiritual Love

1. Divine Love:

- Divine love is the unconditional, all-encompassing love of a higher power for all creation. It is a love that transcends human limitations and embraces all beings with compassion and grace.

- Experiencing divine love often involves surrendering to the divine will, trusting in the higher power's wisdom, and opening one's heart to receive and share this love.

2. Transcendence and Unity:

- Spiritual love often involves a sense of transcendence and unity, where individuals feel connected to something greater than themselves. This connection fosters a sense of oneness with the universe and all living beings.

- Practices that cultivate this sense of unity include meditation, prayer, and rituals that honor the interconnectedness of all life.

Expressions of Spiritual Love in Various Traditions

1. Christianity:

- In Christianity, spiritual love is expressed through the concept of agape, the selfless, unconditional love of God for humanity. Christians are called to emulate this love in their relationships with others.

- Key Practices: Prayer, worship, reading and meditating on the Bible, and acts of charity and service.

- Example: The teachings of Jesus Christ emphasize loving God with all one's heart and loving one's neighbor as oneself (Matthew 22:37-39).

2. Islam:

- In Islam, spiritual love is expressed through the love and devotion to Allah. Muslims believe that Allah's love and mercy encompass all creation, and they strive to live in accordance with His will.

- Key Practices: Salah (prayer), reciting and reflecting on the Quran, fasting during Ramadan, and performing acts of charity (Zakat).

- Example: The Quran emphasizes the compassionate and merciful nature of Allah, and Muslims are encouraged to embody these qualities in their interactions with others (Quran 49:10).

3. Hinduism:

- In Hinduism, spiritual love is expressed through bhakti, the devotional love and worship of the divine. Bhakti yoga is the path of devotion, where individuals seek to unite with God through love and devotion.

- Key Practices: Bhakti yoga, chanting mantras, participating in rituals and ceremonies, and reading sacred texts like the Bhagavad Gita.

- Example: The Bhagavad Gita teaches that devotion to God, expressed through selfless service and love, leads to spiritual liberation (Bhagavad Gita 9:22).

4. Buddhism:

- In Buddhism, spiritual love is expressed through metta, or loving-kindness. Metta is a boundless and unconditional love that extends to all beings, promoting compassion and empathy.

- Key Practices: Metta meditation, mindfulness, following the Noble Eightfold Path, and engaging in compassionate actions.

- Example: The Buddha taught the practice of metta meditation to cultivate loving-kindness and compassion for oneself and others (Sutta Nipata 1.8).

5. Judaism:

- In Judaism, spiritual love is expressed through the love of God and the love of others. The Shema prayer encapsulates the central tenet of loving God with all one's heart, soul, and might.

- Key Practices: Prayer, studying the Torah, observing the mitzvot (commandments), and performing acts of kindness (gemilut hasadim).

- Example: The Torah teaches the importance of loving one's neighbor as oneself (Leviticus 19:18) and emphasizes the compassionate nature of God.

6. Sufism:

- Sufism, the mystical branch of Islam, emphasizes the experience of divine love and union with God. Sufis seek to purify their hearts and attain spiritual closeness to God through love and devotion.

- Key Practices: Dhikr (remembrance of God), poetry, music, and dance (such as the whirling dervishes), and following the guidance of a spiritual teacher (Murshid).

- Example: The poetry of Rumi, a renowned Sufi mystic, often speaks of divine love and the longing for union with the Beloved (God).

Cultivating Spiritual Love in Daily Life

1. Daily Devotional Practices:

- Incorporating daily devotional practices into your routine helps maintain a constant connection with the divine. These practices can include prayer, meditation, reading sacred texts, and reflecting on spiritual teachings.

- Exercise: Set aside dedicated time each day for your chosen devotional practices. Create a sacred space in your home where you can engage in these activities without distractions.

2. Mindfulness and Presence:

- Practicing mindfulness and being present in the moment fosters a deeper awareness of the divine presence in everyday life. Mindfulness helps cultivate a sense of gratitude and reverence for the sacred in all experiences.

- Exercise: Practice mindfulness by focusing on your breath, observing your surroundings, and being fully present in your daily activities. Reflect on the presence of the divine in each moment.

3. Acts of Compassion and Service:

- Engaging in acts of compassion and service expresses spiritual love in action. Serving others selflessly and with love reflects the divine qualities of kindness and mercy.

- Exercise: Identify opportunities for acts of service in your community. Volunteer your time, offer support to those in need, and perform random acts of kindness.

4. Gratitude and Appreciation:

- Cultivating gratitude and appreciation for the blessings in your life strengthens your connection with the divine. Acknowledging the gifts and experiences provided by a higher power fosters a sense of humility and love.

- Exercise: Keep a gratitude journal where you regularly write down things you are grateful for. Reflect on how these blessings connect you to the divine.

5. Spiritual Reflection and Contemplation:

- Taking time for spiritual reflection and contemplation deepens your understanding of divine love and its presence in your life. Contemplative practices help integrate spiritual insights into daily living.

- Exercise: Engage in regular reflection and contemplation. Use questions such as "How do I experience divine love in my life?" and "How can I express this love to others?" to guide your reflections.

The Transformative Power of Spiritual Love

1. Inner Peace and Fulfillment:

- Experiencing spiritual love brings a profound sense of inner peace and fulfillment. It helps individuals find meaning and purpose beyond material pursuits, leading to a more balanced and contented life.

- Reflect on the moments when you have felt a deep sense of spiritual connection and how these experiences have brought peace and fulfillment.

2. Strengthening Resilience:

- Spiritual love provides strength and resilience during challenging times. Trusting in a higher power's love and guidance can help individuals navigate difficulties with grace and courage.

- Reflect on how your faith and spiritual practices have supported you during times of adversity. Consider how this connection can continue to provide strength.

3. Fostering Compassion and Unity:

- Spiritual love fosters compassion and a sense of unity with others. Recognizing the divine presence in all beings promotes empathy, understanding, and a commitment to the well-being of all.

- Reflect on how spiritual love has influenced your interactions with others. Consider ways to deepen your practice of compassion and unity in your daily life.

Experiencing spiritual love connects us with a higher power and enriches our lives with meaning purpose, and inner peace. By exploring the expressions of spiritual love in various traditions and incorporating devotional practices, mindfulness, and acts of compassion into our daily lives, we can cultivate a deeper connection with the divine. This connection fosters resilience, compassion, and a sense of unity with all beings, ultimately leading to a more loving and harmonious world.

As we continue our exploration of love in this book, we will delve into other forms of love, including familial, romantic, and self-love. Through this journey, we can learn how to harness the power of love to heal, transform, and uplift ourselves and those around us, ultimately leading to a more loving and compassionate world.

PRACTICING LOVE IN EVERYDAY LIFE

Practicing Love in Everyday Life: Incorporating Spiritual Principles of Love, Compassion, and Forgiveness into Our Daily Lives

Living a life infused with love, compassion, and forgiveness can transform our everyday experiences and relationships. These spiritual principles are not confined to religious or sacred contexts; they can be integrated into our daily routines, interactions, and decisions. In this chapter, we will explore how to practice love in everyday life by incorporating these principles into our thoughts, actions, and relationships, fostering a more harmonious and fulfilling existence.

The Principle of Love

1. Unconditional Love:

- Unconditional love means loving without expecting anything in return. It is selfless and given freely, embodying the essence of spiritual love.

- Exercise: Practice unconditional love by performing acts of kindness for others without expecting anything in return. Examples include helping a neighbor, volunteering, or simply offering a listening ear.

2. Loving Yourself:

- Self-love is the foundation for loving others. It involves recognizing your own worth, treating yourself with kindness, and prioritizing your well-being.

- Exercise: Engage in self-care activities that nurture your body, mind, and spirit. This can include taking time for relaxation, pursuing hobbies, and setting healthy boundaries.

3. Expressing Love:

- Expressing love through words and actions strengthens relationships and fosters connection. Regularly communicating love and appreciation to those around you creates a positive and supportive environment.

- Exercise: Make a habit of expressing love and appreciation to your family, friends, and colleagues. Simple gestures such as saying "I love you," writing a heartfelt note, or giving a hug can make a significant impact.

The Principle of Compassion

1. Empathy and Understanding:

- Compassion starts with empathy, the ability to understand and share the feelings of others. By putting ourselves in others' shoes, we can respond with kindness and support.

- Exercise: Practice active listening in conversations. Focus on understanding the other person's perspective and validate their feelings without judgment.

2. Acts of Kindness:

- Compassionate acts, no matter how small, can brighten someone's day and foster a sense of connection. These acts can be spontaneous or planned, but they always come from a place of genuine care.

- Exercise: Perform random acts of kindness regularly. Examples include paying for someone's coffee, leaving a kind note for a coworker, or offering to help a neighbor with their groceries.

3. Serving Others:

- Service is a powerful expression of compassion. By dedicating time and effort to help others, we contribute to the well-being of our communities and the world.

- Exercise: Find opportunities to serve others in your community. This can be through volunteering at a local charity, participating in community clean-up events, or supporting a friend in need.

The Principle of Forgiveness

1. Letting Go of Grudges:

- Holding onto grudges and resentment harms us more than it does the other person. Forgiveness is a conscious decision to release these negative emotions and move forward with a lighter heart.

- Exercise: Reflect on any grudges or resentments you are holding. Write a letter of forgiveness (you don't have to send it) to express your feelings and let go of the negativity.

2. Forgiving Yourself:

- Self-forgiveness is just as important as forgiving others. Acknowledge your mistakes, learn from them, and treat yourself with the same compassion you would offer a friend.

- Exercise: Identify any areas where you need to forgive yourself. Write a list of affirmations to remind yourself that everyone makes mistakes and deserves forgiveness.

3. Rebuilding Trust:

- Forgiveness is the first step in rebuilding trust in relationships. Open communication and consistent actions help restore trust and strengthen the bond.

- Exercise: If someone has wronged you and you choose to forgive them, engage in an open conversation about your feelings. Discuss steps to rebuild trust and ensure both parties are committed to the process.

Integrating Spiritual Principles into Daily Life

1. Mindfulness and Presence:

- Being present in the moment allows us to fully experience and appreciate our interactions and surroundings. Mindfulness helps us respond with love, compassion, and forgiveness.

- Exercise: Practice mindfulness by taking a few moments each day to focus on your breath and observe your thoughts without judgment. Bring this awareness into your daily activities and interactions.

2. Daily Reflection:

- Reflecting on our actions and intentions helps us stay aligned with our values and principles. Daily reflection fosters self-awareness and growth.

- Exercise: Set aside time each evening to reflect on your day. Consider how you demonstrated love, compassion, and forgiveness, and identify areas for improvement.

3. Gratitude Practice:

- Cultivating gratitude shifts our focus to the positive aspects of life and fosters a sense of appreciation. Gratitude enhances our ability to love and connect with others.

- Exercise: Keep a gratitude journal where you write down three things you are grateful for each day. Reflect on how these blessings connect you to others and the divine.

4. Setting Intentions:

- Setting intentions helps us approach each day with purpose and mindfulness. Intentions guide our actions and interactions, keeping us focused on living out our spiritual principles.

- Exercise: Each morning, set an intention for the day related to love, compassion, or forgiveness. For example, "Today, I will approach every interaction with kindness and understanding."

5. Engaging in Spiritual Practices:

- Regular spiritual practices such as prayer, meditation, and reading sacred texts reinforce our connection to a higher power and remind us of our commitment to spiritual principles.

- Exercise: Incorporate spiritual practices into your daily routine. This can be as simple as a few minutes of meditation in the morning or reading a passage from a sacred text before bed.

The Impact of Practicing Love in Everyday Life

1. Strengthening Relationships:

- Consistently practicing love, compassion, and forgiveness strengthens our relationships. These principles foster trust, understanding, and a sense of connection.

- Reflect on how these practices have positively impacted your relationships. Consider areas where you can deepen your commitment to these principles.

2. Enhancing Personal Well-Being:

- Living in alignment with spiritual principles enhances our mental and emotional well-being. It brings a sense of peace, fulfillment, and resilience.

- Reflect on how practicing love, compassion, and forgiveness has improved your well-being. Identify areas where you can further integrate these principles into your life.

3. Creating a Positive Ripple Effect:

- Our actions influence those around us, creating a ripple effect of positivity and kindness. By embodying love, compassion, and forgiveness, we inspire others to do the same.

- Reflect on how your actions have inspired others. Consider ways to expand your influence and continue spreading love and compassion.

Practicing love in everyday life by incorporating spiritual principles of love, compassion, and forgiveness transforms our relationships, enhances our well-being, and creates a more harmonious world. By consistently embodying these principles in our thoughts, actions, and interactions, we can foster deeper connections, inspire positive change, and live more fulfilling lives.

As we continue our exploration of love in this book, we will delve into other forms of love, including familial, romantic, and self-love. Through this journey, we can learn how to harness the power of love to heal, transform, and uplift ourselves and those around us, ultimately leading to a more loving and compassionate world.

FINDING MEANING AND PURPOSE

Finding Meaning and Purpose: How Spiritual Love Can Provide Us with a Sense of Purpose and Direction in Life

Spiritual love transcends the material world and connects us with a higher purpose. It provides a sense of meaning and direction, guiding our actions and decisions. This chapter explores how spiritual love can provide us with a sense of purpose and direction in life, using Bible verses as references with expository Bible study and commentary.

Understanding Spiritual Love

1. The Nature of Spiritual Love:

- Spiritual love is an unconditional, selfless love that reflects the nature of God. It is a love that transcends human limitations and embraces all of creation.

- In 1 John 4:8, the Bible states, "Whoever does not love does not know God, because God is love." This verse emphasizes that love is at the core of God's nature and our relationship with Him.

2. The Source of Spiritual Love:

- The source of spiritual love is God Himself. His love is the foundation of our existence and the guiding principle for our lives.

- In Romans 5:5, the Bible says, "And hope does not put us to shame, because God's love has been poured out into our hearts through the Holy Spirit, who has been given to us." This verse highlights that God's love is bestowed upon us through the Holy Spirit.

Spiritual Love and Purpose

1. Created for a Purpose:

- The Bible teaches that each of us is created with a unique purpose and plan. Understanding and embracing this purpose is central to living a fulfilling life.

- In Jeremiah 29:11, it is written, "For I know the plans I have for you," declares the Lord, "plans to prosper you and not to harm you, plans to give you hope and a future." This verse reassures us that God has a specific plan for each of our lives, filled with hope and purpose.

2. Called to Love and Serve:

- One of the fundamental purposes of our lives is to love and serve others. This calling reflects the selfless love of Christ and fulfills God's commandments.

- In Matthew 22:37-39, Jesus teaches, "Love the Lord your God with all your heart and with all your soul and with all your mind.' This is the first and greatest commandment. And the second is like it: 'Love your neighbor as yourself.'" These verses emphasize that loving God and loving others are the greatest commandments, guiding our actions and purpose.

Finding Direction Through Spiritual Love

1. Guidance from the Holy Spirit:

- The Holy Spirit provides guidance and direction in our lives, helping us align our actions with God's will and purpose.

- In John 16:13, Jesus promises, "But when he, the Spirit of truth, comes, he will guide you into all the truth. He will not speak on his own; he will speak only what he hears, and he will tell you what is yet to come." This verse highlights the role of the Holy Spirit in guiding us towards truth and purpose.

ways submit to him, and he will make your paths straight." This verse emphasizes the importance of trusting in God and seeking His guidance in all aspects of life.

Practical Steps to Find Meaning and Purpose Through Spiritual Love

1. Daily Prayer and Reflection:

- Regular prayer and reflection help us stay connected to God and discern His will for our lives. It is through this intimate communication with God that we find clarity and direction.

- Exercise: Set aside time each day for prayer and reflection. Ask God to reveal His purpose for your life and listen for His guidance.

2. Studying Scripture:

- Studying the Bible provides insight into God's character, His promises, and His plans for us. Scripture is a source of wisdom and direction.

- Exercise: Commit to a regular Bible study routine. Choose passages that speak to your need for direction and meditate on their meaning and application in your life.

3. Serving Others:

- Serving others is a practical expression of spiritual love and a way to fulfill God's purpose. It aligns our actions with the teachings of Christ and brings fulfillment and joy.

- Exercise: Look for opportunities to serve in your community, church, or workplace. Acts of service can range from volunteering to simple acts of kindness.

4. Cultivating Gratitude:

- Gratitude helps us recognize and appreciate God's blessings and the opportunities He provides. It shifts our focus from what we lack to what we have, fostering a positive and purposeful outlook.

- Exercise: Keep a gratitude journal where you regularly write down things you are thankful for. Reflect on how these blessings align with God's purpose for your life.

5. Seeking Wise Counsel:

- Seeking advice and counsel from spiritually mature individuals can provide valuable insight and encouragement. Mentors, pastors, and trusted friends can help us discern God's will and make informed decisions.

- Exercise: Identify individuals in your life who exemplify spiritual maturity and wisdom. Reach out to them for guidance and support in your journey.

Examples of Biblical Figures Who Found Purpose Through Spiritual Love

1. Abraham:

- Abraham's life was marked by his faith and obedience to God's calling. Despite uncertainties, he trusted God's promises and followed His direction.

- In Genesis 12:1-3, God calls Abraham to leave his homeland and promises to make him a great nation.

Abraham's journey of faith exemplifies how trusting in God's plan can lead to a purposeful life.

2. Moses:

- Moses found his purpose in leading the Israelites out of Egypt and towards the Promised Land. Despite his initial reluctance, he embraced God's calling and became a pivotal leader.

- In Exodus 3:10, God says to Moses, "So now, go. I am sending you to Pharaoh to bring my people the Israelites out of Egypt." Moses' life demonstrates how God equips and directs us to fulfill His purposes.

3. Paul:

- The Apostle Paul experienced a dramatic transformation and dedicated his life to spreading the Gospel. His writings and missionary journeys had a profound impact on the early church and continue to inspire believers.

- In Acts 9:15-16, God tells Ananias about Paul, "Go! This man is my chosen instrument to proclaim my name to the Gentiles and their kings and to the people of Israel. I will show him how much he must suffer for my name." Paul's life illustrates the power of God's calling and the fulfillment found in serving His mission.

The Impact of Spiritual Love on Personal Growth

1. Strengthening Faith:

- Spiritual love deepens our relationship with God and strengthens our faith. It provides the foundation for trust and reliance on His guidance.

- Reflect on how your faith has grown through experiences of spiritual love and how this growth has influenced your sense of purpose.

2. Fostering Inner Peace:

- Knowing and following God's purpose brings a sense of inner peace and contentment. It alleviates the anxiety of uncertainty and aligns our lives with a higher calling.

- Reflect on moments when you felt a deep sense of peace and fulfillment, knowing you were aligned with God's will.

3. Encouraging Resilience:

- Spiritual love empowers us to persevere through challenges and setbacks. Trusting in God's plan gives us the resilience to overcome obstacles and remain steadfast in our purpose.

- Reflect on how spiritual love has helped you navigate difficult times and how it has strengthened your resolve.

Finding meaning and purpose through spiritual love involves connecting with God's unconditional love, understanding His plans for us, and aligning our lives with His will. By engaging in daily prayer, studying Scripture, serving others, cultivating gratitude, and seeking wise counsel, we can discern and fulfill our divine purpose. The examples of biblical figures like Abraham, Moses, and Paul inspire us to trust in God's guidance and embrace the journey He has set before us.

As we continue our exploration of love in this book, we will delve into other forms of love, including familial, romantic, and self-love. Through this journey, we can learn how to harness the power of love to heal, transform, and uplift ourselves and those around us, ultimately leading to a more loving and compassionate world.

CHAPTER 07

WHAT DOES LOVE DO IN OUR LIVES

Love is one of the most powerful forces in the human experience. It transcends boundaries, heals wounds, and inspires us to reach our highest potential. This chapter explores the transformative power of love, examining how it can heal emotional wounds, mend broken relationships, inspire kindness and generosity, and motivate personal growth. Love, in its various forms, enriches our lives, providing purpose and meaning.

1. Healing Emotional Wounds

Love has an extraordinary capacity to heal emotional wounds. Whether the love comes from family, friends, or a partner, it can offer solace and comfort during difficult times.

- Emotional Support: Being loved provides a sense of security and support. Knowing that someone cares deeply for us can alleviate feelings of loneliness and despair.

- Validation and Understanding: Love validates our experiences and emotions. When someone truly understands and accepts us, it helps to heal past traumas and reduce emotional pain.

- Encouraging Vulnerability: In a loving environment, we feel safe to express our true selves and be vulnerable. This openness is essential for emotional healing and personal growth.

2. Mending Broken Relationships

Love can mend broken relationships, whether they are romantic, familial, or platonic. The process of reconciliation often begins with love and leads to stronger, more resilient bonds.

- Forgiveness and Reconciliation: Love encourages forgiveness, allowing us to let go of grudges and past hurts. This forgiveness is crucial for repairing and rebuilding relationships.

- Communication and Understanding: Love fosters open and honest communication. When we communicate with love, we are more likely to understand each other's perspectives and resolve conflicts.

- Commitment and Effort: Love requires a commitment to making relationships work. This commitment motivates us to put in the necessary effort to mend and strengthen our connections.

3. Inspiring Acts of Kindness and Generosity

Love inspires acts of kindness and generosity, creating a ripple effect that can positively impact entire communities.

- Empathy and Compassion: Love enhances our ability to empathize with others. This empathy drives us to act with compassion, helping those in need and making the world a better place.

- Altruism: Love often motivates altruistic behavior, where we act selflessly for the benefit of others. This can range from small acts of kindness to significant contributions to society.

- Building Community: Acts of kindness and generosity, inspired by love, help to build strong and supportive communities. These actions foster a sense of belonging and mutual support.

4. Motivating Personal Growth and Self-Improvement

Love can be a powerful motivator for personal growth and self-improvement. It inspires us to become better versions of ourselves.

- Encouragement and Support: The love and support of others can encourage us to pursue our goals and dreams. Knowing that someone believes in us can boost our confidence and determination.

- Self-Love and Acceptance: Love helps us to cultivate self-love and acceptance. When we love ourselves, we are more likely to engage in behaviors that promote our well-being and personal growth.

- Setting Positive Examples: Loving relationships often provide positive role models. Seeing the strengths and qualities in those we love can inspire us to develop similar attributes in ourselves.

5. Providing Purpose and Meaning

Love enriches our lives by providing purpose and meaning. It connects us to something greater than ourselves.

- Sense of Belonging: Love gives us a sense of belonging and connection. This feeling of being part of something larger than ourselves adds depth and meaning to our lives.

- Motivating Purposeful Actions: Love motivates us to act with purpose, whether it's taking care of our families, contributing to our communities, or pursuing our passions.

- Spiritual Connection: For many, love is a spiritual experience that connects them to a higher power or the greater good. This spiritual connection provides a profound sense of purpose and fulfillment.

Love transforms our lives in profound ways. It heals emotional wounds, mends broken relationships, inspires acts of kindness and generosity, and motivates personal growth and self-improvement. Love enriches our lives by providing purpose and meaning, making it a driving force that shapes our experiences and connections. By understanding and embracing the transformative power of love, we can lead richer, more fulfilling lives and create a more compassionate and connected world.

CHAPTER 08

WHY ARE OUR PARENTS' LOVE IMPORTANT? THE LESSONS LEARNED

The love we receive from our parents is a cornerstone of our development and overall well-being. It serves as the first form of love we experience, deeply influencing our psychological, emotional, and social growth. Parental love provides the essential foundation upon which we build our lives, shaping our beliefs, values, and attitudes. This chapter explores the critical role of parental love, examining its impact on our sense of security, emotional resilience, self-perception, and interpersonal relationships.

1. Providing Security and Stability

One of the most crucial aspects of parental love is the sense of security and stability it offers, especially during our formative years.

- Sense of Safety: Parental love creates a safe environment where children feel protected and cared for. This sense of safety is essential for healthy emotional and psychological development.

- Consistent Support: Consistency in love and support from parents helps children develop a sense of stability. Knowing that they can rely on their parents provides a strong foundation for exploring the world and taking risks.

- Emotional Anchor: Parents serve as emotional anchors, offering comfort and reassurance during times of distress. This emotional grounding is vital for developing trust and confidence.

2. Fostering Emotional Resilience

Emotional resilience, the ability to cope with stress and adversity, is significantly influenced by parental love.

- Emotional Regulation: Children learn to regulate their emotions by observing and interacting with their parents. Parental love helps them develop coping mechanisms to manage their feelings effectively.

- Supportive Environment: A loving and supportive home environment allows children to express their emotions freely and seek comfort when needed, building resilience.

- Encouragement and Validation: Parental encouragement and validation reinforce a child's ability to persevere through challenges. Knowing they are loved unconditionally boosts their self-esteem and resilience.

3. Shaping Beliefs, Values, and Attitudes

Parental love plays a pivotal role in shaping our core beliefs, values, and attitudes.

- Role Modeling: Parents are primary role models. Their actions and attitudes towards love, kindness, honesty, and integrity profoundly influence their children's values.

- Moral Development: Through loving guidance and discipline, parents instill moral values and ethical principles in their children. This foundation influences how they perceive right and wrong throughout life.

- Worldview Formation: Parental love and teachings shape a child's worldview, including their attitudes towards themselves, others, and the world around them.

4. Influencing Self-Perception

The way parents love and treat their children significantly impacts their self-perception and self-worth.

- Positive Reinforcement: Loving parents provide positive reinforcement, helping children develop a healthy self-image and confidence in their abilities.

- Unconditional Acceptance: Feeling unconditionally loved by parents fosters self-acceptance and reduces the fear of failure. It helps children understand that their worth is not dependent on their achievements.

- Identity Formation: Parental love contributes to a child's identity formation. Supportive parents encourage their children to explore their interests and develop a strong sense of self.

5. Laying the Foundation for Healthy Relationships

The love we receive from our parents sets the stage for how we approach relationships later in life.

- Attachment Style: Early interactions with parents influence attachment styles, which affect how individuals relate to others in adulthood. Secure attachment with parents typically leads to healthier, more stable relationships.

- Communication Skills: Loving parents model effective communication, teaching their children how to express themselves and listen to others. These skills are crucial for building and maintaining healthy relationships.

- Empathy and Compassion: Experiencing parental love teaches empathy and compassion, key components of meaningful and supportive relationships with others.

The love of parents is a profound and enduring force that shapes who we are and who we become. It provides the security and stability necessary for healthy development, fosters emotional resilience, shapes our beliefs and values, influences our self-perception, and lays the foundation for healthy relationships. Recognizing the importance of parental love helps us appreciate its impact on our lives and underscores the need to cultivate and cherish this foundational relationship. Through understanding and valuing parental love, we can better navigate our personal growth and relationships, ultimately leading to a more fulfilled and balanced life.

CHAPTER 09

GOD IS LOVE – GOD'S UNCONDITIONAL LOVE TO HUMANITY

The declaration "God is love" found in the Bible encapsulates the essence of God's character and His relationship with humanity. God's love is unconditional, boundless, and transformative. It is the foundation upon which the Christian faith is built and offers a profound source of comfort, guidance, and inspiration. In this chapter, we will explore the nature of God's unconditional love, its manifestations in the Bible, and its implications for our lives.

The Nature of God's Unconditional Love

1. God's Love is Unconditional:

- God's love is not based on our actions, worthiness, or merit. It is given freely and unconditionally.

- Romans 5:8: "But God demonstrates his own love for us in this: While we were still sinners, Christ died for us."

- Commentary: This verse highlights that God's love does not depend on our behavior or righteousness. It is a gift given to us even when we are undeserving.

2. God's Love is Everlasting:

- God's love is eternal and unchanging. It is a constant presence in our lives, providing stability and assurance.

- Jeremiah 31:3: "The Lord appeared to us in the past, saying: 'I have loved you with an everlasting love; I have drawn you with unfailing kindness.'"

- Commentary: God's love is not fleeting or conditional. It is an everlasting commitment to us, reflecting His eternal nature.

3. God's Love is Sacrificial:

- The ultimate expression of God's love is the sacrifice of Jesus Christ for the salvation of humanity.

- John 3:16: "For God so loved the world that he gave his one and only Son, that whoever believes in him shall not perish but have eternal life."

- Commentary: This verse underscores the depth of God's love, demonstrated through the sacrificial giving of His Son to redeem humanity.

Manifestations of God's Love in the Bible

1. Creation:

- God's love is evident in the act of creation. He created the world and humanity out of love, desiring a relationship with His creation.

- Genesis 1:27: "So God created mankind in his own image, in the image of God he created them; male and female he created them."

- Commentary: Being made in God's image signifies the special relationship and love God has for humanity, reflecting His desire for us to share in His nature.

2. Covenants:

- Throughout the Bible, God makes covenants with His people, promising to be their God and to bless them. These covenants are expressions of His steadfast love and commitment.

- Genesis 9:13: "I have set my rainbow in the clouds, and it will be the sign of the covenant between me and the earth."

- Commentary: The covenant with Noah, symbolized by the rainbow, represents God's promise of protection and His ongoing relationship with creation.

3. Deliverance:

- God's love is manifested in His acts of deliverance and salvation. He repeatedly rescues His people from bondage and oppression.

- Exodus 6:6: "Therefore, say to the Israelites: 'I am the Lord, and I will bring you out from under the yoke of the Egyptians. I will free you from being slaves to them, and I will redeem you with an outstretched arm and with mighty acts of judgment.'"

- Commentary: God's deliverance of the Israelites from Egypt is a powerful demonstration of His love and commitment to their well-being and freedom.

4. Provision:

- God's love is shown through His provision and care for our needs. He sustains us and provides for our physical, emotional, and spiritual needs.

- Matthew 6:26: "Look at the birds of the air; they do not sow or reap or store away in barns, and yet your heavenly Father feeds them. Are you not much more valuable than they?"

- Commentary: This verse reassures us of God's attentive care and provision, reflecting His loving commitment to our well-being.

5. Forgiveness:

- God's love is evident in His willingness to forgive our sins and restore our relationship with Him.

- 1 John 1:9: "If we confess our sins, he is faithful and just and will forgive us our sins and purify us from all unrighteousness."

- Commentary: God's readiness to forgive emphasizes His loving nature, offering us grace and a path to reconciliation.

Implications of God's Unconditional Love for Our Lives

1. Security and Assurance:

- Knowing that God's love is unconditional and everlasting provides us with security and assurance, freeing us from fear and anxiety.

- Romans 8:38-39: "For I am convinced that neither death nor life, neither angels nor demons, neither the present nor the future, nor any powers, neither height nor depth, nor anything else in all creation, will be able to separate us from the love of God that is in Christ Jesus our Lord."

- Commentary: This passage reassures us that nothing can separate us from God's love, offering us profound comfort and confidence.

2. Purpose and Identity:

- God's love gives us a sense of purpose and identity, affirming our worth and calling as His beloved children.

- 1 John 3:1: "See what great love the Father has lavished on us, that we should be called children of God! And that is what we are!"

- Commentary: Understanding ourselves as children of God, loved and valued by Him, shapes our identity and purpose in life.

3. Motivation to Love Others:

- Experiencing God's love compels us to love others with the same unconditional and sacrificial love.

- 1 John 4:11: "Dear friends, since God so loved us, we also ought to love one another."

- Commentary: This verse calls us to reflect God's love in our interactions with others, fostering a community of compassion and selflessness.

4. Encouragement in Difficult Times:

- God's love provides encouragement and strength during difficult times, reminding us that we are never alone.

- Psalm 46:1: "God is our refuge and strength, an ever-present help in trouble."

- Commentary: In times of trouble, God's love is a source of refuge and strength, offering us unwavering support and hope.

5. Transformation and Growth:

- God's love transforms us, helping us grow in character, faith, and holiness. It is through His love that we are continually being made new.

- 2 Corinthians 5:17: "Therefore, if anyone is in Christ, the new creation has come: The old has gone, the new is here!"

- Commentary: God's love leads to our transformation, guiding us toward a life that reflects His righteousness and grace.

God's unconditional love is the foundation of our faith and the ultimate expression of His character. It is a love that is sacrificial, everlasting, and transformative, impacting every aspect of our lives. By understanding and embracing God's love, we find security, purpose, and motivation to love others. This profound love offers us encouragement in difficult times and guides our growth and transformation.

As we continue our exploration of love in this book, we will delve into other forms of love, including familial, romantic, and self-love. Through this journey, we can learn how to harness the power of love to heal, transform, and uplift ourselves and those around us, ultimately leading to a more loving and compassionate world.

CHAPTER 10

CAN LOVE BRING PEACE TO HUMANITY

Love has long been heralded as a powerful force for good, capable of transforming individuals and societies. But can love truly bring peace to humanity? This chapter explores the potential of love to foster peace on personal, communal, and global levels. We will examine biblical principles, historical examples, and practical applications of love as a means to achieve lasting peace.

The Biblical Foundation of Love and Peace

1. The Command to Love:

- The Bible commands believers to love one another, emphasizing that love is foundational to a harmonious and peaceful existence.

- John 13:34-35: "A new command I give you: Love one another. As I have loved you, so you must love one another. By this everyone will know that you are my disciples, if you love one another."

- Commentary: Jesus' command to love one another is not just a moral directive but a transformative principle that fosters unity and peace among His followers.

2. Love as the Fulfillment of the Law:

- Love is presented in the Bible as the fulfillment of the law, encompassing all other commandments and leading to a righteous and peaceful life.

- Romans 13:10: "Love does no harm to a neighbor. Therefore love is the fulfillment of the law."

- Commentary: When love guides our actions, it naturally leads to behavior that promotes peace and well-being for others.

3. The Peace of Christ:

- Jesus offers a peace that transcends human understanding, rooted in His love and sacrifice.

- John 14:27: "Peace I leave with you; my peace I give you. I do not give to you as the world gives. Do not let your hearts be troubled and do not be afraid."

- Commentary: The peace that Christ offers is deeply intertwined with His love, providing a sense of security and calm that can permeate our lives and relationships.

Historical Examples of Love Bringing Peace

1. The Civil Rights Movement:

- The Civil Rights Movement in the United States, led by figures like Martin Luther King Jr., exemplifies how love and nonviolence can bring about significant social change and peace.

- King's philosophy of nonviolent resistance was deeply rooted in Christian love and the teachings of Jesus.

- Example: The Montgomery Bus Boycott and the March on Washington were peaceful protests driven by a commitment to love and justice, resulting in substantial progress toward racial equality.

2. Reconciliation in South Africa:

- The end of apartheid in South Africa and the subsequent reconciliation process led by Nelson Mandela and Desmond Tutu demonstrated the power of love and forgiveness in healing a divided nation.

- The Truth and Reconciliation Commission focused on restorative justice, emphasizing understanding, love, and forgiveness over retribution.

- Example: Mandela's choice to forgive his oppressors and Tutu's insistence on truth-telling and reconciliation fostered a peaceful transition and laid the foundation for a more unified society.

3. Peacebuilding in Northern Ireland:

- The peace process in Northern Ireland, marked by the Good Friday Agreement, involved significant efforts of love, forgiveness, and mutual understanding between conflicting parties.

- Religious leaders and community activists played crucial roles in fostering dialogue and reconciliation.

- Example: The cooperation between Catholic and Protestant leaders, such as John Hume and David Trimble, showcased how love and a commitment to peace can overcome deep-seated animosities.

Practical Applications of Love for Peace

1. Personal Relationships:

- Love in personal relationships fosters understanding, reduces conflict, and promotes harmony.

- Exercise: Practice active listening, empathy, and forgiveness in your relationships. Prioritize open communication and express love through actions and words.

2. Community Building:

- Love within communities encourages cooperation, support, and collective well-being.

- Exercise: Engage in community service, participate in local events, and build relationships with your neighbors. Promote inclusivity and kindness in your community interactions.

3. Conflict Resolution:

- Love-based conflict resolution focuses on understanding, empathy, and finding mutually beneficial solutions.

- Exercise: When faced with conflict, approach the situation with a mindset of love and compassion. Seek to understand the other person's perspective and work towards a resolution that respects both parties' needs.

4. Global Peace Initiatives:

- Love-driven global initiatives promote peace through diplomacy, humanitarian aid, and cultural exchange.

- Exercise: Support international organizations that work towards peace and justice. Advocate for policies that promote global cooperation and humanitarian assistance.

The Transformative Power of Love

1. Healing and Reconciliation:

- Love has the power to heal wounds and foster reconciliation. It allows individuals and communities to move past grievances and build a foundation for lasting peace.

- Reflect on instances where love and forgiveness have led to healing in your life or community. Consider how these principles can be applied more broadly.

2. Building Trust and Cooperation:

- Love builds trust and encourages cooperation, essential components for peaceful coexistence. When people feel loved and valued, they are more likely to collaborate and support one another.

- Reflect on how trust and cooperation have been strengthened through acts of love in your relationships or community.

3. Promoting Justice and Equality:

- Love drives the pursuit of justice and equality, addressing the root causes of conflict and creating a more just and peaceful society.

- Reflect on how love has motivated efforts to promote justice and equality in your life or community. Consider ways to further these efforts.

Challenges and Solutions

1. Overcoming Hatred and Prejudice:

- Challenge: Deep-seated hatred and prejudice can be significant barriers to peace.

- Solution: Promote education, dialogue, and cultural exchange to break down stereotypes and foster understanding. Encourage acts of love and kindness towards those who are different from us.

2. Dealing with Violence and Aggression:

- Challenge: Violence and aggression can escalate conflicts and hinder peace efforts.

- Solution: Advocate for nonviolent conflict resolution methods and support initiatives that address the underlying causes of violence. Promote love and empathy as alternatives to aggression.

3. Addressing Inequality and Injustice:

- Challenge: Inequality and injustice fuel resentment and conflict.

- Solution: Work towards systemic changes that promote equality and justice. Support policies and initiatives that address social, economic, and political disparities.

Love has the profound potential to bring peace to humanity. Through personal relationships, community building, conflict resolution, and global initiatives, love can foster understanding, cooperation, and healing. The biblical principles of love, as well as historical examples, demonstrate that love is a powerful force for good, capable of transforming individuals and societies. By embracing love in our daily lives and promoting it in our interactions and initiatives, we can contribute to a more peaceful and compassionate world. As we continue our exploration of love in this book, let us be inspired to harness the power of love to heal, transform, and uplift ourselves and those around us, ultimately leading to lasting peace and harmony.

CHAPTER 11

LOVE COVERS A MULTITUDE OF SINS

The phrase "love covers a multitude of sins" is a powerful biblical truth that emphasizes the transformative and redemptive power of love. This chapter will explore the meaning and implications of this phrase, examining its biblical context, practical applications, and how love can bring healing and reconciliation in the face of human imperfection.

Biblical Foundation

1. Scriptural Reference:

- The phrase "love covers a multitude of sins" is found in 1 Peter 4:8.

- 1 Peter 4:8: "Above all, love each other deeply, because love covers over a multitude of sins."

- Commentary: This verse highlights the primacy of love in the Christian life. Peter urges believers to love deeply, emphasizing that love has the power to cover sins, fostering forgiveness and unity within the community.

2. Proverbs and Love:

- The concept is also reflected in the Old Testament, particularly in Proverbs.

- Proverbs 10:12: "Hatred stirs up conflict, but love covers over all wrongs."

- Commentary: This proverb contrasts the destructive nature of hatred with the healing power of love. Love, unlike hatred, brings peace and reconciliation by covering wrongs.

Understanding "Covers a Multitude of Sins"

1. Forgiveness and Grace:

- Love covering sins is closely related to forgiveness and grace. It involves forgiving others as an expression of love and extending grace instead of holding onto offenses.

- Ephesians 4:32: "Be kind and compassionate to one another, forgiving each other, just as in Christ God forgave you."

- Commentary: Forgiveness is a practical manifestation of love. When we forgive, we reflect God's love and grace, covering the sins of others and promoting reconciliation.

2. Compassion and Understanding:

- Love also involves showing compassion and understanding towards others' faults and failures. It means choosing to focus on the good in others rather than their shortcomings.

- Colossians 3:13-14: "Bear with each other and forgive one another if any of you has a grievance against someone. Forgive as the Lord forgave you. And over all these virtues put on love, which binds them all together in perfect unity."

- Commentary: Compassion and understanding are essential aspects of love. By bearing with one another and forgiving, we create an environment of unity and support.

3. Peacemaking:

- Love fosters peacemaking, which is essential for resolving conflicts and covering sins. It involves actively seeking to restore relationships and bring harmony.

- Matthew 5:9: "Blessed are the peacemakers, for they will be called children of God."

- Commentary: Peacemaking is a vital expression of love. It requires humility, patience, and a commitment to reconciliation, reflecting the heart of God.

Practical Applications

1. In Personal Relationships:

- Love covers sins in personal relationships by promoting forgiveness, understanding, and peacemaking. It involves choosing to see the best in others and letting go of past hurts.

- Exercise: Reflect on any personal relationships where there may be unresolved conflicts or lingering resentments. Make a conscious effort to forgive, show compassion, and seek reconciliation.

2. In Community and Church:

- Within a community or church, love fosters unity and harmony by covering the sins and shortcomings of its members. It creates an environment where people feel accepted and valued despite their imperfections.

- Exercise: Engage in community-building activities that promote love and unity. Volunteer, participate in small groups, and support others in their spiritual journey.

3. In the Workplace:

- In the workplace, love can transform relationships and foster a positive environment. It involves treating colleagues with respect, showing kindness, and resolving conflicts peacefully.

- Exercise: Practice acts of kindness and understanding towards your colleagues. Address conflicts with a spirit of reconciliation and seek to build a supportive work environment.

Overcoming Challenges to Love

1. Dealing with Hurt and Betrayal:

- Loving others, especially when they have wronged us, can be challenging. It requires overcoming hurt and betrayal through the power of forgiveness and grace.

- Luke 6:27-28: "But to you who are listening I say: Love your enemies, do good to those who hate you, bless those who curse you, pray for those who mistreat you."

- Commentary: Jesus' teaching on loving our enemies emphasizes the radical nature of Christian love. It challenges us to extend love even in the face of mistreatment.

2. Letting Go of Resentment:

- Holding onto resentment and bitterness can hinder our ability to love and forgive. It is essential to release these negative emotions and allow love to heal our hearts.

- Hebrews 12:15: "See to it that no one falls short of the grace of God and that no bitter root grows up to cause trouble and defile many."

- Commentary: Bitterness can take root and cause harm if not addressed. By letting go of resentment, we create space for love and grace to flourish.

3. Cultivating a Heart of Love:

- Developing a heart of love involves intentional practices such as prayer, reflection, and acts of kindness. It requires a commitment to embodying the love of Christ in our daily lives.

- 1 Corinthians 13:4-7: "Love is patient, love is kind. It does not envy, it does not boast, it is not proud. It does not dishonor others, it is not self-seeking, it is not easily angered, it keeps no record of wrongs. Love does not delight in evil but rejoices with the truth. It always protects, always trusts, always hopes, always perseveres."

- Commentary: This passage from 1 Corinthians provides a comprehensive description of love's attributes. Reflecting on these qualities can inspire us to cultivate a heart of love.

The Transformative Power of Love

1. Healing and Restoration:

- Love has the power to heal wounds and restore broken relationships. It brings reconciliation and fosters an environment of trust and support.

- Reflect on relationships that have been healed through love and forgiveness. Consider how you can apply these principles in your current relationships.

2. Promoting Unity and Harmony:

. - Love unites individuals and communities, promoting harmony and peace. It bridges gaps and fosters a sense of belonging and mutual respect.

- Reflect on how love has promoted unity in your community or church. Consider ways to further these efforts and encourage others to do the same.

3. Reflecting God's Character:

- By loving others and covering their sins, we reflect God's character and His unconditional love for humanity. It is a testimony of our faith and a powerful witness to the world.

- Reflect on how your actions and attitudes reflect God's love. Consider how you can be a more effective witness of His love in your daily life.

The biblical principle that "love covers a multitude of sins" underscores the transformative and redemptive power of love. By embodying forgiveness, compassion, and peacemaking, we can foster healing, unity, and reconciliation in our relationships and communities. Overcoming challenges to love requires intentional effort and reliance on God's grace, but the rewards are profound and far-reaching. As we continue our exploration of love in this book, let us be inspired to harness the power of love to heal, transform, and uplift ourselves and those around us, ultimately leading to a more loving and compassionate world.

CHAPTER 12

HOW CAN WE USE LOVE TO HEAL THE WORLD AND BROKEN HEARTS?

Love is a powerful force with the potential to heal wounds, mend broken hearts, and transform the world. In a world filled with conflict, pain, and suffering, love offers a pathway to healing and reconciliation. This chapter explores how we can use love to heal both on a personal level and within the broader context of society. By examining practical applications, biblical principles, and real-life examples, we will uncover the ways love can bring about profound healing and restoration.

The Healing Power of Love

1. Personal Healing:

- Love has the ability to heal personal wounds and mend broken hearts. It provides comfort, support, and a sense of belonging.

- Psalm 147:3: "He heals the brokenhearted and binds up their wounds."

- Commentary: God's love is a source of healing for the brokenhearted. When we experience and extend love, we participate in this divine healing process.

2. Healing Relationships:

- Love can restore and strengthen relationships that have been damaged by conflict, misunderstanding, or betrayal.

- Colossians 3:13-14: "Bear with each other and forgive one another if any of you has a grievance against someone. Forgive as the Lord forgave you. And over all these virtues put on love, which binds them all together in perfect unity."

- Commentary: Forgiveness and love are essential for healing relationships. Love binds us together and promotes unity.

3. Societal Healing:

- Love can address societal wounds such as injustice, discrimination, and inequality. It promotes empathy, understanding, and collective well-being.

- Micah 6:8: "He has shown you, O mortal, what is good. And what does the Lord require of you? To act justly and to love mercy and to walk humbly with your God."

- Commentary: Acting justly, loving mercy, and walking humbly are expressions of love that contribute to societal healing.

Practical Applications of Love for Healing

1. Active Listening and Empathy:

- Active listening and empathy are foundational to love's healing power. They involve being fully present and understanding the feelings and experiences of others.

- Exercise: Practice active listening in your interactions. Focus on understanding the other person's perspective without judgment or interruption.

2. Acts of Kindness and Support:

- Small acts of kindness and support can have a significant impact on someone's healing journey. These acts demonstrate love and care in tangible ways.

- Exercise: Perform random acts of kindness regularly. Offer help, encouragement, and support to those in need.

3. Forgiveness and Reconciliation:

- Forgiveness is a powerful act of love that can heal deep wounds. It involves letting go of resentment and seeking reconciliation.

- Exercise: Reflect on any grudges or unresolved conflicts in your life. Take steps towards forgiveness and seek to restore broken relationships.

4. Community Building:

- Building strong, supportive communities fosters a sense of belonging and collective healing. It involves creating environments where everyone feels valued and accepted.

- Exercise: Engage in community-building activities such as volunteering, organizing events, and supporting local initiatives. Promote inclusivity and kindness within your community.

5. Advocacy and Social Justice:

- Love motivates us to advocate for justice and address systemic issues that cause suffering. It calls us to stand with the marginalized and oppressed.

- Exercise: Support organizations and movements that promote social justice. Use your voice and resources to advocate for change and address inequalities.

Biblical Examples of Love Bringing Healing

1. The Good Samaritan:

- The parable of the Good Samaritan illustrates how love can heal and restore. The Samaritan's compassionate actions towards a wounded stranger demonstrate the power of love in action.

- Luke 10:33-34: "But a Samaritan, as he traveled, came where the man was; and when he saw him, he took pity on him. He went to him and bandaged his wounds, pouring on oil and wine. Then he put the man on his own donkey, brought him to an inn and took care of him."

- Commentary: The Good Samaritan's actions exemplify love's capacity to heal physical and emotional wounds through compassion and care.

2. Jesus Healing the Sick:

- Jesus' ministry was marked by acts of healing motivated by love and compassion. His healing miracles restored health and brought hope to many.

- Matthew 14:14: "When Jesus landed and saw a large crowd, he had compassion on them and healed their sick."

- Commentary: Jesus' healing miracles reflect His deep love and compassion. They serve as examples of how love can bring physical, emotional, and spiritual healing.

3. Joseph Forgiving His Brothers:

- Joseph's forgiveness of his brothers, who had sold him into slavery, illustrates how love and forgiveness can heal family wounds and restore relationships.

- Genesis 50:20-21: "You intended to harm me, but God intended it for good to accomplish what is now being done, the saving of many lives. So then, don't be afraid. I will provide for you and your children." And he reassured them and spoke kindly to them.

- Commentary: Joseph's forgiveness and provision for his brothers demonstrate how love can overcome betrayal and lead to reconciliation and healing.

Overcoming Barriers to Love

1. Dealing with Fear and Vulnerability:

- Fear and vulnerability can hinder our ability to love and be loved. Overcoming these barriers requires courage and trust.

- 1 John 4:18: "There is no fear in love. But perfect love drives out fear because fear has to do with punishment. The one who fears is not made perfect in love."

- Commentary: Perfect love drives out fear, enabling us to love freely and fully. Trusting in God's love empowers us to overcome fear and embrace vulnerability.

2. Addressing Anger and Resentment:

- Anger and resentment can block the flow of love and prevent healing. Letting go of these negative emotions is essential for love to bring healing.

- Ephesians 4:31-32: "Get rid of all bitterness, rage and anger, brawling and slander, along with every form of malice. Be kind and compassionate to one another, forgiving each other, just as in Christ God forgave you."

- Commentary: Releasing anger and embracing kindness and compassion allows love to heal and restore relationships.

3. Cultivating a Heart of Love:

- Developing a heart of love involves intentional practices such as prayer, reflection, and acts of kindness. It requires a commitment to embodying the love of Christ in our daily lives.

- 1 Corinthians 13:4-7: "Love is patient, love is kind. It does not envy, it does not boast, it is not proud. It does not dishonor others, it is not self-seeking, it is not easily angered, and it keeps no record of wrongs. Love does not delight in evil but rejoices with the truth. It always protects, always trusts, always hopes, always perseveres."

- Commentary: Reflecting on these qualities can inspire us to cultivate a heart of love, enabling us to bring healing to others.

Real-Life Examples of Love Bringing Healing

1. Community Support during Crises:

- In times of crisis, communities often come together in love and support, providing aid, comfort, and healing to those affected.

- Example: During natural disasters, such as hurricanes or earthquakes, community members and organizations mobilize to provide relief and support, demonstrating love in action.

2. Reconciliation and Forgiveness:

- Stories of reconciliation and forgiveness illustrate how love can heal deep wounds and restore relationships.

- Example: The story of Immaculée Ilibagiza, a survivor of the Rwandan genocide, who forgave those who killed her family, highlights the power of love and forgiveness to bring healing and peace.

3. Acts of Kindness and Generosity:

- Simple acts of kindness and generosity can have a profound impact on individuals, bringing hope and healing to those in need.

- Example: The work of organizations like Habitat for Humanity, which builds homes for those in need, exemplifies how love and generosity can transform lives and communities.

Love has the extraordinary power to heal both individual hearts and the broader world. By practicing active listening and empathy, performing acts of kindness and support, embracing forgiveness and reconciliation, building strong communities, and advocating for justice, we can harness the healing power of love. Overcoming barriers such as fear, anger, and resentment requires courage and trust in God's love. Real-life examples and biblical teachings underscore that love is not just a feeling but an active, transformative force that can bring profound healing and restoration.

As we continue our exploration of love in this book, let us be inspired to harness the power of love to heal, transform, and uplift ourselves and those around us, ultimately leading to a more loving and compassionate world.

CHAPTER 13

HOW CAN WE USE LOVE TO UNITE THE BROKEN FAMILIE?

Families are the foundational units of society, providing support, love, and a sense of belonging. However, many families experience fractures and brokenness due to conflicts, misunderstandings, and various life challenges. This chapter explores how love can be a powerful force to unite and heal broken families. By examining biblical principles, practical strategies, and real-life examples, we will discover ways to foster reconciliation, understanding, and unity within families.

The Biblical Foundation of Family Unity

1. The Importance of Love:

- Love is the cornerstone of healthy and united families. The Bible emphasizes the importance of love in building strong family bonds.

- Colossians 3:14: "And over all these virtues put on love, which binds them all together in perfect unity."

- Commentary: Love is the glue that holds families together, promoting harmony and unity.

2. Forgiveness and Reconciliation:

- Forgiveness is essential for healing family wounds and restoring relationships. The Bible teaches the importance of forgiving others as God forgives us.

- Ephesians 4:32: "Be kind and compassionate to one another, forgiving each other, just as in Christ God forgave you."

- Commentary: Forgiveness paves the way for reconciliation and the rebuilding of trust within the family.

3. Honoring and Respecting Each Other:

- Mutual honor and respect are crucial for maintaining healthy family relationships. The Bible instructs family members to honor and respect one another.

- Romans 12:10: "Be devoted to one another in love. Honor one another above yourselves."

- Commentary: Honoring and respecting each other fosters an environment of love and understanding, essential for family unity.

Practical Strategies for Uniting Broken Families

1. Open and Honest Communication:

- Effective communication is key to resolving conflicts and fostering understanding. Families must prioritize open and honest conversations.

- Exercise: Set aside regular family meetings where everyone can share their thoughts and feelings. Encourage active listening and empathy.

2. Practicing Forgiveness:

- Forgiveness is a powerful act of love that can heal deep wounds. It involves letting go of past hurts and moving forward with compassion.

- Exercise: Reflect on any unresolved conflicts or grudges within the family. Make a conscious effort to forgive and seek reconciliation.

3. Showing Appreciation and Gratitude:

- Regularly expressing appreciation and gratitude strengthens family bonds. It helps family members feel valued and loved.

- Exercise: Create a family tradition of sharing gratitude. During meals or gatherings, have each member share something they appreciate about one another.

4. Spending Quality Time Together:

- Quality time fosters connection and strengthens relationships. Engaging in activities together creates positive memories and reinforces family unity.

- Exercise: Plan regular family activities such as game nights, outings, or vacations. Ensure that these activities involve meaningful interactions and shared experiences.

5. Supporting Each Other:

- Providing emotional and practical support during challenging times demonstrates love and commitment. It reinforces the sense of being part of a supportive family unit.

- Exercise: Identify ways to support each other in daily life. This can include helping with chores, offering a listening ear, or providing encouragement.

Real-Life Examples of Love Uniting Families

1. Reconciliation After Estrangement:

- Families can experience reconciliation even after long periods of estrangement through intentional efforts of love and forgiveness.

- Example: A father and daughter who had been estranged for years began to reconcile after the daughter reached out with a heartfelt letter expressing her desire to rebuild their relationship. Through open communication and mutual forgiveness, they gradually restored their bond.

2. Overcoming Tragedy Together:

- Tragedies can either further fracture a family or bring them closer together. Love and support can help families navigate and heal from difficult times.

- Example: A family who lost a loved one in a tragic accident found strength in their faith and each other. By leaning on one another, sharing their grief, and supporting each other, they emerged stronger and more united.

3. Blended Families:

- Blending families after remarriage presents unique challenges, but love and intentional efforts can create a harmonious family unit.

- Example: A couple with children from previous marriages worked hard to unite their blended family. They held regular family meetings, encouraged open communication, and created new family traditions. Over time, love and mutual respect fostered a sense of unity and belonging.

Biblical Examples of Family Unity

1. The Prodigal Son:

- The parable of the prodigal son illustrates the power of forgiveness and unconditional love in restoring family unity.

- Luke 15:20: "So he got up and went to his father. But while he was still a long way off, his father saw him and was filled with compassion for him; he ran to his son, threw his arms around him, and kissed him."

- Commentary: The father's unconditional love and willingness to forgive his wayward son led to reconciliation and the restoration of their relationship.

2. Joseph and His Brothers:

- Joseph's forgiveness of his brothers, who had betrayed him, exemplifies how love and forgiveness can heal deep family wounds.

- Genesis 45:4-5: "Then Joseph said to his brothers, 'Come close to me.' When they had done so, he said, 'I am your brother Joseph, the one you sold into Egypt! And now, do not be distressed and do not be angry with yourselves for selling me here, because it was to save lives that God sent me ahead of you.'"

- Commentary: Joseph's decision to forgive and reconcile with his brothers brought healing and unity to their family.

3. Ruth and Naomi:

- Ruth's unwavering love and loyalty to her mother-in-law Naomi demonstrate the strength of family bonds and the importance of supporting one another.

- Ruth 1:16: "But Ruth replied, 'Don't urge me to leave you or to turn back from you. Where you go I will go, and where you stay I will stay. Your people will be my people and your God my God.'"

- Commentary: Ruth's dedication to Naomi highlights the power of love and loyalty in maintaining family unity even in the face of adversity.

Overcoming Barriers to Family Unity

1. Dealing with Resentment and Anger:

- Resentment and anger can hinder family unity. Overcoming these emotions requires forgiveness and a commitment to moving forward.

- Ephesians 4:31-32: "Get rid of all bitterness, rage and anger, brawling and slander, along with every form of malice. Be kind and compassionate to one another, forgiving each other, just as in Christ God forgave you."

- Commentary: Letting go of negative emotions and embracing kindness and compassion fosters a positive and healing environment within the family.

2. Addressing Communication Breakdowns:

\- Poor communication can lead to misunderstandings and conflicts. Improving communication skills is essential for resolving issues and maintaining unity.

- James 1:19: "My dear brothers and sisters, take note of this: Everyone should be quick to listen, slow to speak and slow to become angry."

- Commentary: Effective communication involves active listening, thoughtful responses, and controlling anger, all of which contribute to healthier family dynamics.

3. Navigating Differences:

- Differences in opinions, values, and personalities can create tension within families. Embracing diversity and finding common ground are key to unity.

- Romans 12:16: "Live in harmony with one another. Do not be proud, but be willing to associate with people of low position. Do not be conceited."

- Commentary: Humility and a willingness to embrace differences help create a harmonious family environment.

Love is a transformative force that can unite and heal broken families. By practicing open communication, forgiveness, appreciation, quality time, and support, families can foster unity and overcome challenges. Biblical teachings and real-life examples demonstrate that love, when applied intentionally and consistently, has the power to restore and strengthen family bonds. As we continue our exploration of love in this book, let us be inspired to harness the power of love to heal, transform, and uplift our families, ultimately leading to a more loving and compassionate world.

CHAPTER 14

WHY IS FAMILY LOVE IMPORTANT TO YOU?

Family love is one of the most profound and enduring types of love we experience. It forms the bedrock of our emotional and social lives, providing a sense of belonging, support, and identity. This chapter explores why family love is important, highlighting its role in personal development, emotional stability, social cohesion, and overall well-being. Understanding the significance of family love can help us appreciate its value and inspire us to nurture and cherish our family bonds.

1. Providing a Sense of Belonging

One of the primary reasons family love is so important is the sense of belonging it provides.

- Unconditional Acceptance: Family members often offer unconditional love and acceptance. Knowing that you are valued and accepted for who you are, without conditions, fosters a deep sense of belonging.

- Identity and Roots: Family provides a sense of identity and continuity. Understanding your family's history, traditions, and values helps you feel connected to something larger than yourself.

- Shared Experiences: Families share experiences and memories that create a unique bond. These shared moments, both good and bad, strengthen the sense of belonging and togetherness.

2. Emotional Support and Stability

Family love offers crucial emotional support and stability throughout life's ups and downs.

- Emotional Anchor: Family members often serve as emotional anchors, offering support, understanding, and comfort during difficult times. This emotional safety net is essential for mental health and resilience.

- Encouragement and Motivation: Loving families provide encouragement and motivation. They celebrate successes and offer support during failures, helping individuals to persevere and achieve their goals.

- Conflict Resolution: Within a loving family, conflicts can be resolved in a supportive and understanding manner.

This helps to build emotional resilience and teaches effective conflict-resolution skills.

3. Promoting Personal Growth and Development

Family love plays a significant role in personal growth and development.

- Values and Morals: Families instill values and morals that guide behavior and decision-making. These foundational principles shape character and influence life choices.

- Role Models: Family members often serve as role models. Observing their actions and attitudes provides valuable lessons in responsibility, integrity, and compassion.

- Learning Environment: A loving family creates a nurturing environment for learning and growth. It encourages exploration, curiosity, and the development of skills and talents.

4. Strengthening Social Cohesion

Family love extends beyond the individual, contributing to social cohesion and community strength.

- Community Building: Families often form the nucleus of communities. Strong family bonds can lead to active and engaged communities where members support each other.

- Civic Responsibility: Families teach civic responsibility and the importance of contributing to society.

This sense of duty and community service is often passed down through generations.

- Support Networks: Extended family networks provide additional layers of support, creating a robust social safety net. This interconnectedness fosters a sense of security and communal strength.

5. Enhancing Overall Well-being

The love and support from family significantly enhance overall well-being and quality of life.

- Physical Health: Research shows that individuals with strong family connections tend to have better physical health. Family love can lead to healthier lifestyle choices and provide support during health challenges.

- Mental Health: Emotional support from family is crucial for mental health. It helps to reduce stress, anxiety, and depression, contributing to a more balanced and fulfilling life.

- Life Satisfaction: A loving family contributes to higher life satisfaction. The sense of connection, purpose, and support from family members leads to a more fulfilling and content life.

Family love is a vital component of a fulfilling life. It provides a sense of belonging, emotional support, and stability, promotes personal growth, strengthens social cohesion, and enhances overall well-being. Understanding the importance of family love helps us appreciate the value of our family bonds and inspires us to nurture and cherish these relationships. By fostering a loving and supportive family environment, we contribute to our own happiness and the well-being of those around us, creating a more compassionate and connected world.

CHAPTER 15

WHY IS GOD'S LOVE IMPORTANT TO ALL OF US?

God's love is a concept that transcends religious boundaries, offering profound implications for human existence and spiritual growth. It provides comfort, guidance, and a sense of purpose, influencing how we perceive ourselves and interact with the world. This chapter explores the importance of God's love, delving into its nature and the concept of Rema Love, a divine expression of love that profoundly impacts our lives.

1. What is God's Love?

God's love is often described as unconditional, infinite, and all-encompassing. It is a foundational concept in many religious traditions, signifying a love that surpasses human understanding and limitations.

- Unconditional Love: Unlike human love, which can be conditional and fleeting, God's love is constant and unwavering. It is not based on our actions or worthiness but is freely given.

- Sacrificial Love: In Christianity, God's love is epitomized by the sacrifice of Jesus Christ, who gave His life for humanity's redemption. This sacrificial aspect underscores the depth and selflessness of divine love.

- Personal and Intimate: God's love is personal, extending to each individual uniquely. It involves a deep, intimate relationship between the Creator and the created, offering comfort, guidance, and a sense of belonging.

- Transformative Power: God's love has the power to transform lives, bringing healing, restoration, and new purpose. It encourages individuals to live according to higher principles of compassion, forgiveness, and service.

2. The Importance of God's Love

God's love is vital for several reasons, deeply impacting our spiritual, emotional, and social lives.

- Sense of Worth and Identity: Understanding and accepting God's love helps individuals recognize their intrinsic worth and value. This divine love assures us that we are cherished and valued beyond human standards.

- Guidance and Purpose: God's love provides a moral and spiritual compass, guiding us toward righteous living and purposeful existence. It inspires us to seek truth, justice, and compassion in our daily lives.

- Comfort and Hope: In times of suffering and uncertainty, God's love offers comfort and hope. It reassures us that we are not alone and that a higher power cares for us deeply.

- Foundation for Human Relationships: God's love sets a standard for how we should love others. It teaches us to extend grace, forgiveness, and unconditional love in our relationships, fostering a more compassionate and harmonious society.

3. What is Rema Love?

Rema Love is a term that may not be widely recognized across all religious traditions but is often understood within certain Christian contexts as a specific, profound expression of God's love.

- Divine Revelation: Rema Love refers to a direct, personal revelation of God's love to an individual. It is often experienced as a deep, spiritual insight or moment of clarity where God's love is felt powerfully and personally.

- Personal Encounter: This type of love involves a personal encounter with God that transcends intellectual understanding, reaching into the heart and soul. It often results in a profound sense of peace, joy, and transformation.

- Guidance and Empowerment: Rema Love can provide specific guidance and empowerment for individuals, revealing God's will and purpose for their lives in a clear and personal way.

- Healing and Restoration: Experiences of Rema Love often bring healing to emotional and spiritual wounds, restoring individuals to a state of wholeness and renewed purpose.

4. The Impact of God's Love on Our Lives

Understanding and embracing God's love can have a transformative impact on our lives, influencing our behavior, relationships, and overall well-being.

- Inner Peace and Joy: Experiencing God's love brings inner peace and joy that transcends circumstances. This deep sense of contentment is rooted in the assurance of being loved unconditionally.

- Strength and Resilience: God's love provides strength and resilience in the face of life's challenges. Knowing that we are loved by a higher power gives us the courage to persevere and overcome difficulties.

- Motivation for Goodness: God's love inspires us to act with kindness, compassion, and integrity. It motivates us to serve others selflessly and to make positive contributions to the world.

- Spiritual Growth: Embracing God's love fosters spiritual growth and maturity. It encourages us to deepen our relationship with God, seeking to understand and live out divine principles in our daily lives.

God's love is a profound and transformative force that holds immense significance for all of us. It provides a sense of worth, guidance, comfort, and purpose, shaping our lives in meaningful ways. The concept of Rema Love further illustrates the personal and intimate nature of God's love, offering direct, revelatory experiences that can deeply impact our spiritual journey. By understanding and embracing God's love, we can lead more fulfilling, compassionate, and purposeful lives, drawing closer to the divine and to each other in meaningful and lasting ways.

CONCLUSION

Summary of Key Points

Throughout this book, we have explored the multifaceted nature of love and its profound impact on our lives. We began by understanding the essence of love, delving into its various forms, including romantic love, familial love, platonic love, and self-love. We examined the biological and psychological foundations of love, recognizing the intricate interplay of hormones, neurotransmitters, emotions, and mental processes that define our experiences of love.

We discussed the importance of love in relationships, highlighting how it fosters trust, communication, and mutual respect, and how it contributes to the health and longevity of these relationships. We explored how love functions within society, acting as a catalyst for social cohesion, resilience, and justice. We looked at the transformative power of love, its ability to heal emotional wounds, mend broken relationships, inspire acts of kindness, and motivate personal growth.

We delved into the significance of parental love, understanding its critical role in shaping our development, emotional resilience, self-perception, and relational skills. We also reflected on the importance of God's love, recognizing its unconditional nature and its profound influence on our spiritual and emotional well-being.

The Power of Love in Humanity

Love is a driving force in humanity, capable of transforming individuals and communities. It is the foundation of our most cherished relationships and the glue that holds societies together. Love has the power to break down barriers, heal divisions, and create a more compassionate and just world.

- Healing Power: Love heals. It mends the broken and soothes the wounded, offering comfort and hope. Whether through the tender care of a parent, the support of a friend, or the grace of divine love, it provides the balm that heals our deepest hurts.

- Transformational Force: Love transforms. It motivates us to grow, to strive for better, and to become the best versions of ourselves. It inspires acts of selflessness, courage, and kindness that ripple out, creating positive change.

- Social Cohesion: Love unites. It fosters empathy, understanding, and mutual respect, which are essential for building strong, resilient communities. Love encourages us to look beyond our differences and work together for the common good.

Encouragement for Loving One Another

In a world that can often seem divided and tumultuous, the need for love is greater than ever. As we conclude this exploration of love, let us be reminded of its boundless potential to enrich and transform our lives and the lives of those around us.

- Practice Self-Love: Begin with yourself. Embrace self-compassion and self-acceptance. Recognize your worth and nurture your well-being. When you love yourself, you are better equipped to love others.

- Cherish Your Relationships: Invest time and effort in your relationships. Communicate openly, show appreciation, and be there for your loved ones. Strong, loving relationships are a source of joy and support.

- Extend Kindness and Compassion: Let love guide your actions. Practice kindness, empathy, and generosity. Small acts of love can have a profound impact, creating a ripple effect that spreads positivity and hope.

- Seek to Understand and Forgive: Approach conflicts with a loving heart. Strive to understand others' perspectives and be willing to forgive. Love has the power to heal divisions and build bridges.

- Embrace Divine Love: For those who believe, draw strength and guidance from the love of God. Let this divine love inspire you to live a life of compassion, service, and integrity.

By embracing and nurturing love in its many forms, we can create a world that is more compassionate, just, and connected. Let love be the guiding principle in your life, and witness the profound difference it can make in your own journey and in the lives of those around you. Love is not just an emotion; it is a powerful force that has the potential to transform humanity.